Competitive Strategies for Continuing Education

Clifford Baden, *Editor*
Harvard University

NEW DIRECTIONS FOR CONTINUING EDUCATION
GORDON G. DARKENWALD, *Editor-in-Chief*
Rutgers University

ALAN B. KNOX, *Consulting Editor*
University of Wisconsin

Number 35, Fall 1987

Paperback sourcebooks in
The Jossey-Bass Higher Education Series

Jossey-Bass Inc., Publishers
San Francisco • London

Clifford Baden (ed.).
Competitive Strategies for Continuing Education.
New Directions for Continuing Education, no. 35.
San Francisco: Jossey-Bass, 1987.

New Directions for Continuing Education
Gordon G. Darkenwald, *Editor-in-Chief*
Alan B. Knox, *Consulting Editor*

Copyright © 1987 by Jossey-Bass Inc., Publishers
and
Jossey-Bass Limited

Copyright under International, Pan American, and Universal
Copyright Conventions. All rights reserved. No part of
this issue may be reproduced in any form—except for brief
quotation (not to exceed 500 words) in a review or professional
work—without permission in writing from the publishers.

New Directions for Continuing Education is published quarterly
by Jossey-Bass Inc., Publishers (publication number USPS 493-930).
Second-class postage paid at San Francisco, California, and at
additional mailing offices. POSTMASTER: Send address changes to
Jossey-Bass Inc., Publishers, 433 California Street, San Francisco,
California 94104.

Editorial correspondence should be sent to the Editor-in-Chief,
Gordon G. Darkenwald, Graduate School of Education, Rutgers
University, 10 Seminary Place, New Brunswick, New Jersey 08903.

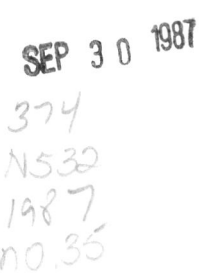

Library of Congress Catalog Card Number LC 85-644750

International Standard Serial Number ISSN 0195-2242

International Standard Book Number ISBN 1-55542-951-3

Cover art by WILLI BAUM

Manufactured in the United States of America

Ordering Information

The paperback sourcebooks listed below are published quarterly and can be ordered either by subscription or single copy.

Subscriptions cost $48.00 per year for institutions, agencies, and libraries. Individuals can subscribe at the special rate of $36.00 per year *if payment is by personal check*. (Note that the full rate of $48.00 applies if payment is by institutional check, even if the subscription is designated for an individual.) Standing orders are accepted.

Single copies are available at $11.95 when payment accompanies order. (California, New Jersey, New York, and Washington, D.C., residents please include appropriate sales tax.) For billed orders, cost per copy is $11.95 plus postage and handling.

Substantial discounts are offered to organizations and individuals wishing to purchase bulk quantities of Jossey-Bass sourcebooks. Please inquire.

Please note that these prices are for the academic year 1987-88 and are subject to change without notice. Also, some titles may be out of print and therefore not available for sale.

To ensure correct and prompt delivery, all orders must give either the *name of an individual* or an *official purchase order number*. Please submit your order as follows:

Subscriptions: specify series and year subscription is to begin.
Single Copies: specify sourcebook code (such as, CE1) and first two words of title.

Mail orders for United States and Possessions, Australia, New Zealand, Canada, Latin America, and Japan to:
  Jossey-Bass Inc., Publishers
  433 California Street
  San Francisco, California 94104

Mail orders for all other parts of the world to:
  Jossey-Bass Limited
  28 Banner Street
  London EC1Y 8QE

New Directions for Continuing Education Series
Gordon G. Darkenwald, *Editor-in-Chief*
Alan B. Knox, *Consulting Editor*

CE1 *Enhancing Proficiencies of Continuing Educators,* Alan B. Knox
CE2 *Programming for Adults Facing Mid-Life Change,* Alan B. Knox
CE3 *Assessing the Impact of Continuing Education,* Alan B. Knox

CE4	*Attracting Able Instructors of Adults,* M. Alan Brown, Harlan G. Copeland
CE5	*Providing Continuing Education by Media and Technology,* Martin N. Chamberlain
CE6	*Teaching Adults Effectively,* Alan B. Knox
CE7	*Assessing Educational Needs of Adults,* Floyd C. Pennington
CE8	*Reaching Hard-to-Reach Adults,* Gordon G. Darkenwald, Gordon A. Larson
CE9	*Strengthening Internal Support for Continuing Education,* James C. Votruba
CE10	*Advising and Counseling Adult Learners,* Frank R. DiSilvestro
CE11	*Continuing Education for Community Leadership,* Harold W. Stubblefield
CE12	*Attracting External Funds for Continuing Education,* John H. Buskey
CE13	*Leadership Strategies for Meeting New Challenges,* Alan B. Knox
CE14	*Programs for Older Adults,* Morris A. Okun
CE15	*Linking Philosophy and Practice,* Sharan B. Merriam
CE16	*Creative Financing and Budgeting,* Travis Shipp
CE17	*Materials for Teaching Adults: Selection, Development, and Use,* John P. Wilson
CE18	*Strengthening Connections Between Education and Performance,* Stanley M. Grabowski
CE19	*Helping Adults Learn How to Learn,* Robert M. Smith
CE20	*Educational Outreach to Select Adult Populations,* Carol E. Kasworm
CE21	*Meeting Educational Needs of Young Adults,* Gordon G. Darkenwald, Alan B. Knox
CE22	*Designing and Implementing Effective Workshops,* Thomas J. Sork
CE23	*Realizing the Potential of Interorganizational Cooperation,* Hal Beder
CE24	*Evaluation for Program Improvement,* David Deshler
CE25	*Self-Directed Learning: From Theory to Practice,* Stephen Brookfield
CE26	*Involving Adults in the Educational Process,* Sandra H. Rosenblum
CE27	*Problems and Prospects in Continuing Professional Education,* Ronald M. Cervero, Craig L. Scanlan
CE28	*Improving Conference Design and Outcomes,* Paul J. Ilsley
CE29	*Personal Computers and the Adult Learner,* Barry Heermann
CE30	*Experiential and Simulation Techniques for Teaching Adults,* Linda H. Lewis
CE31	*Marketing Continuing Education,* Hal Beder
CE32	*Issues in Adult Career Counseling,* Juliet V. Miller, Mary Lynne Musgrove
CE33	*Responding to the Educational Needs of Today's Workplace,* Ivan Charner, Catherine A. Rolzinski
CE34	*Technologies for Learning Outside the Classroom,* John A. Niemi, Dennis D. Gooler

Contents

Editor's Notes 1
Clifford Baden

1. **Competitive Strategy in Continuing Education** 5
Clifford Baden
Each continuing education provider must choose a single strategy that is consonant with its skills, interests, and resources.

2. **Competitive Strategy in a Fragmented Field** 19
Clifford Baden
Most providers have accommodated themselves to reaching a small share of the local market; a few are discovering new ways to compete for students.

3. **Strategic Market Planning in Conglomerate Continuing Education Programs** 31
James P. Pappas
The large, multi-program university continuing education unit must employ certain strategies in order to retain its market leadership.

4. **Competitive Strategy in Continuing Professional Education** 45
John F. Azzaretto
A commitment to the concept of service identifies the most successful providers of continuing professional education.

5. **Contracting with Business and Industry** 59
Richard B. Fischer
Colleges and universities have certain competitive advantages as they pursue training contracts with business and industry.

6. **Telecommunications as an Element of Competitive Strategy** 71
Barbara Gellman-Buzin
As geographical boundaries disappear and students' expectations grow, telecommunications offers new strategic opportunities to continuing education providers.

7. **Collaboration as a Competitive Strategy** 85
Hal Beder
To prosper in a competitive marketplace, a provider must often incur risks; collaboration can be a useful strategy for reducing risk.

8. Competitive Strategy: Themes and Issues 97
Clifford Baden

Several suggestions for creating a sustainable competitive advantage emerge from the chapters of this sourcebook.

Index 103

Editor's Notes

The phrase *competitive strategy* may make some readers feel uncomfortable. At best, it may connote Machiavellian plotting to gain the upper hand. At worst, it may connote aggressive, unprincipled maneuvering to drive competitors out of the marketplace. Neither of these connotations is intended here.

This sourcebook starts from the premise that the field of continuing education is increasing in complexity as the number of providers increases. Most providers entering the field do so with the expectation that they will remain and prosper in the continuing education arena. In order to do so, each provider must find a way to be consistently attractive to learners. Each provider must choose a strategy or pattern of policies and decisions that will create and sustain a competitive advantage—a strategy that will allow the provider to thrive in a crowded marketplace.

Chapter One begins by describing some of the important variables in any provider's strategy in continuing education. Some of these variables (pricing policies, risk orientation) result from conscious choices. Other variables (financial flexibility, the relationship with a parent organization) are a function of history and circumstances. The combination of these variables determines a provider's strengths and weaknesses and indicates where it is likely to be a strong competitor and where it is vulnerable to competition. The chapter concludes with a look at three generic approaches to strategy that are likely to lead to success over the long term.

Chapter Two examines the peculiarities of the continuing education field and the ways in which the field influences the success of providers' strategies. The field is fragmented. It is characterized by many providers, each serving a small, predominantly local, share of the market. The chapter explains why the field is structured in this way and how most providers have adapted their strategies to this kind of environment. Some, however, have not accepted the constraints imposed by the field and have discovered new ways to compete—ways that may reshape the nature of competition in continuing education in the near future.

In Chapter Three, Pappas considers the strategies used by conglomerate providers—the continuing education divisions of large universities—that often play a dominant role in the local market. He explains why these providers are able to achieve market leadership positions and what strategies will be useful to them in maintaining leadership in today's competitive marketplace.

In Chapter Four, Azzaretto examines competitive strategy in continuing professional education. He proposes a five-part competitive planning model, emphasizing that the most successful providers of continuing professional education are those who adopt a consistent service orientation. He concludes with a review of strategic options that have proved successful in this particular field.

Continuing education for business and industry is another area that has attracted the attention of many providers in recent years. Fischer, in Chapter Five, considers the perspective of colleges and universities and asks what strategies they should use to secure a part of this growing market for themselves. He also emphasizes the importance of a strong consumer service orientation, and he proposes internal policies that will be necessary for an effective, consumer-responsive strategy.

Gellman-Buzin, in Chapter Six, looks at the potential of telecommunications for changing the nature of the continuing education landscape. She describes several regional and national models of telecommunications use, and she discusses what advantages each model offers to providers. The options are many, and growing; the costs and complexity can seem daunting, but for providers who can envision reaching new populations of learners, telecommunications offers exciting possibilities.

Many of the telecommunications models involve collaboration among several providers. Collaboration is the subject of Chapter Seven. Beder argues that collaboration is an important and useful option in formulating a competitive strategy. He suggests the different circumstances in which a provider's long-term strategic interests can be well served by joining forces with other organizations or with other providers.

Chapter Eight recapitulates the important themes that emerge throughout the book. It suggests that there will be many opportunities for innovation and marked expansion in the coming years. It also emphasizes the importance of consistency and a learner-centered mission.

In fact, every one of the chapter authors in this sourcebook emphasizes the importance of serving learners' needs as the sine qua non of any competitive strategy. No strategy will be successful if it does not focus well on meeting learners' needs. The ideal position for a provider is to be able to meet more learners' needs more effectively than other providers. The difficult strategic decisions revolve around how to get to this position: which learners to serve, with what kinds of courses, and with what kinds of operating policies. This volume should be helpful in thinking through these decisions.

Four of my coauthors in this sourcebook are former participants in Harvard University's Institute for the Management of Lifelong Education (MLE). I am grateful for their colleagueship; like all the participants in MLE, they have broadened my understanding of the field of continuing education and have heightened my appreciation of the challenges of leadership.

Clifford Baden
Editor

Clifford Baden is director of Programs in Professional Education at the Harvard Graduate School of Education and director of Harvard's Institute for the Management of Lifelong Education.

In an increasingly competitive environment, what strategies will help providers not only to retain their current positions but also to prosper?

Competitive Strategy in Continuing Education

Clifford Baden

As providers of continuing education look to the future, most see a challenging prospect. The opportunities for creative programming seem endless: weekend schools, courses in shopping centers, contracts with business, industry, and the military, literacy initiatives, delivery options through telecommunications, revivals of the liberal arts, curricula for professional groups, and so on. At the same time, providers acknowledge that there is a changing pattern of competition in the field, with new players and new sponsoring organizations making available to adults a diversity of learning opportunities. Biology courses are offered not only by colleges, universities, and community-based adult education programs but also by botanical gardens and hospitals. Technical updating for industry is available through community colleges, schools of engineering, proprietary schools, professional associations, and in-house training departments. Courses in wine appreciation, seminars in financial planning for women, certificate programs in real estate, one-day sessions on spread-sheet programs—all are promoted by many different providers.

To the extent that providers operate in the same marketplace, they are competitors. The picture is complicated, of course, by the fact that the competitors are so diverse—in their origins, in their personalities, and in their relationships to their parent organizations. As a result, they typically have different goals and different strategies for attracting students. Many of them will also measure success differently.

In an increasingly competitive environment, how can providers of continuing education position themselves to attract and retain an audience of learners for their programs? This is the question this sourcebook will address. (Throughout this volume, *continuing education* is used synonymously with *adult education* to encompass the full range of credit and noncredit learning opportunities.)

Useful approaches to the question can be found in the traditional literature on management. Writers in the field of business policy (Drucker, 1974; Christensen, Andrews, and Bower, 1978; Newman, Logan, and Hegarty, 1985) raise the fundamental questions, What business are we in? What is our distinctive competence? What opportunities match our strengths? What trends favor our position?

Marketing literature (Kotler, 1982; Lovelock, 1984; Lovelock and Weinberg, 1984; Kotler and Fox, 1985) provides other useful insights. With its emphasis on meeting the client's—or the learner's—needs, this literature is particularly helpful in clarifying the concept of market segments. What are useful ways of categorizing and subdividing the total market? If we cannot serve all segments equally well, which can we serve best and how can we communicate with them? What core services does a given market segment need? What ancillary services does it want? How should our programs be priced, promoted, and delivered?

A third group of management experts (Abell and Hammond, 1979; Merson and Qualls, 1979; Andrews, 1980; Shanklin and Ryans, 1985) cites the benefits of strategic planning. These authors typically suggest that an organization begin by identifying important environmental factors and trends. One or more models for analyzing and structuring the environmental data can then be used to develop long-term goals for the organization. Finally, resource allocation models may be employed to help managers move from conceptualization to the implementation of strategy.

More recently, the work of Porter (1980, 1985) articulates the notions of *competitive analysis* and *competitive strategy*. Porter's most useful insight is that the competitors in any field need to know more than just the names of the other competitors. They need to understand the structure of the field itself—who is in it now, to be sure; but also who is likely to enter it, what makes it easy or difficult to get into the field, what economic or structural factors shape competition in the field, and so on. All these forces influence the competitive environment within which organizations operate, and they determine which strategies stand the greatest chances of success.

This sourcebook takes insights from business policy, from marketing, from strategic planning, and from Porter's work on competitive strategy and applies them to the field of continuing education. It suggests ways of looking at the field, it helps to explain many of the field's characteristics, and it raises questions that can help providers better understand themselves and their competitors. Most important, it outlines specific strategies that can lead providers to long-term prosperity.

Strategic Variables

Providers' strategies for entering and competing in the field of continuing education can differ in a variety of dimensions. One way to understand these strategies is to look at the strategic variables differentiating providers. Some variables are the result of deliberate choices, others are a function of history, and still others are structural. Each of the variables discussed below is presented in question form in order to underscore that there is no single right or best response within any of these areas. Different providers have in fact developed highly successful strategies at both extremes of each variable.

Specialization. To what extent does a provider focus its efforts on specific groups of learners? On a given range of course offerings? On a particular geographic market? Some providers have a broad community orientation and adopt a mass-market approach to continuing education. Others focus their programs much more narrowly. In the latter case, a provider that is well respected by a specific clientele may be relatively unknown to the community at large.

Provider Image. To what extent does the provider try to compete by promoting a certain image of itself rather than by competing on the basis of its specific programming decisions? The prestige of the provider (or of its parent organization) can be a powerful selling tool. Some providers use advertising heavily to promote the elite status of the institution. Others distinguish themselves through the services (placement, counseling, and so on) they offer to learners, and their advertising focuses on these services rather than on course offerings. At the other end of the spectrum are providers who concentrate on organizing a series of courses that will attract an audience, and their promotional materials are simply course lists. Many community colleges fall into this category.

Push Versus Pull. Is the provider best at promoting its programs through advertising and direct mail aimed at the individual learner (*push*)? Or does the provider prefer to sell its programs through contracts to group purchasers—corporations, military bases, and so on—that will in turn promote the course offerings to individual learners (*pull*)? The first strategy calls for sensitivity to shifting public tastes and skills in direct-marketing techniques. The second strategy requires intimate knowledge of a few key clients as well as good negotiating skills.

Risk Orientation. How willing is the provider to enter new markets or to develop entirely new programs? How much of the provider's programming each year is new? Is the provider known as an innovator, or is it best at replicating and refining what has already been tried? How is the performance of program developers evaluated? How easy is it to allocate resources within the organization for new undertakings? A provider with a high risk-orientation—which is often supported by the parent organization—is likely to be a strong competitor, willing to move rapidly into new program areas.

Technological Leadership. Does the provider employ state-of-the-art technology in the classroom? Is the provider the first in the community to use satellite or microwave transmission? Are new technologies for learning and teaching used in all programs or only in those that have technology as their subject matter? Or is technology entirely irrelevant to the education sought by the provider's clientele? Is tradition valued more highly, both by the provider and by the learners, than innovation? Do the risks of alienating existing students outweigh the potential advantages of attracting new learners through technology?

Life-Span Integration. To what extent does the provider offer programs to learners throughout their lives rather than at just one period? An example of life-span integration is the professional school that has summer courses to attract high school students, graduate-level degree programs, professional education programs for practitioners in the field, and programs for retired professionals. An integrated range of programs such as this allows the provider to present itself as knowledgeable about all aspects of professional practice. The community education departments of some hospitals, having adopted life-span integration strategies, offer programs for children and adolescents, prospective and new parents, people with specific medical problems, people with aging parents, and so on. One strategic advantage of life-span integration, of course, is that it allows the provider to serve the same client several times and reduces the need to develop new clienteles continually.

Operating Costs. To what extent does the provider seek to minimize costs? The low-cost provider characteristically uses low-overhead office spaces; does not invest in teaching facilities, preferring instead to rent as needed; does not invest in permanent teaching staff; has low-budget publications and promotional materials; and is willing to cancel any course that does not meet predetermined break-even objectives.

Representing the other extreme, the continuing education programs at Harvard's professional schools face unusually high costs because of the university's internal pricing policies and because of the costs prevailing in the Boston area. For these schools, high costs dictate a competitive strategy that includes premium prices supported by a high-quality image. Their competition comes primarily from other schools pursuing a parallel strategy. The high-cost provider is unlikely to challenge the low-cost provider.

Price Policy. What is the provider's relative price position in the continuing education marketplace? Does it try to keep its prices on a par with those charged by others in the same geographic area? Does it consistently seek to position itself as a lower-priced alternative to other providers? Is it willing to price its programs above the market? A provider's price policy will usually be related to such other strategic considerations as cost policy, but it is a distinct variable that should be considered separately.

Service. How many ancillary services does a provider offer? The community education program offering recreational courses at the local high school in the evening may offer no ancillary services at all. In contrast, the community college may offer admissions, academic, career, transfer, and financial counseling; a library, a bookstore, and a student lounge; child care services; and so on. Neither of these strategies is better than the other—both attract students—but different approaches to support services may require very different competitive strategies.

Financial Flexibility. How much financial flexibility does the provider have? How free is it to set tuition levels for each of its course offerings or to negotiate the terms of a contract with a local firm? Does it always have a financial cushion because it is part of a larger organization that can help it through cash-flow crises? Is it free to take surplus revenues from an existing program and invest them in a new program? The ideal of total financial flexibility is relatively rare within the broad spectrum of continuing education providers. Some providers are constrained by very specific financial targets for each course or each program they offer. Others—typically those with a community service orientation—regularly operate at or below their true break-even levels.

Geographical Flexibility. How much flexibility does the provider have in locating its program offerings? Is the provider campus-bound? Is it city-bound? Or can it offer its programs anywhere in the country? In some cases, such as IBM's new high-technology training facility in New York, the provider has no flexibility. Heavy investment in technology typically requires that learners come to a single provider location. At the other extreme, community education programs may have dozens of teaching sites. The Baldwin Park Adult School in California, for example, offers courses in more than forty locations. Between these extremes are providers that rely on telecommunications. Although they quite easily move beyond a single location, their flexibility is limited by the technology required at the learners' location.

Geographical flexibility is also a function of traditions and attitudes. A belief that learning is somehow less credible if it happens off site, away from the provider's home location, is all that limits the flexibility of some providers. Attitudes toward and capacity for site flexibility are important in determining how and where a provider will compete.

Relationship with a Parent Organization. Is the continuing education provider a unit within some larger organization? Parent organizations (as most university-based continuing educators will attest) can be a mixed blessing. On the one hand, they impose requirements and constraints that may limit the provider's ability to respond to new opportunities. On the other hand, parent organizations offer services and resources (usually below market cost), as well as a short-term financial cushion.

The critical consideration for providers with parent organizations is the nature of the relationship between the two. How much autonomy does the continuing education provider have? What is the nature of the reporting relationship? To what extent can the provider influence the goals or policies of the parent organization in support of its own objectives? Does the parent organization set financial targets for the provider, and if so, how do these influence programming decisions? What resources of the parent organization are available to the provider at no cost?

Although there are undoubtedly other strategic variables that could be described, the twelve presented above are among the most important. Together, these variables give the strongest clues to a provider's competitive strategy. The composite picture that emerges indicates strengths and weaknesses, preferred operating styles, and degrees of flexibility in responding to a changing environment. It can also suggest whether new program ideas are likely to provoke retaliation from existing providers, as a couple of examples will illustrate:

> Two teacher-training colleges with fairly similar curricula operated in the same city. College A was the more conservative of the two, with a strong faculty voicing the opinion that on-campus credit-bearing courses were the preferred teaching mode. Recognizing this, College B saw an opportunity to develop part-time, off-campus courses for teachers, located at schools in the surrounding communities and co-sponsored by the teacher's union. And it did so, secure in the belief that College A could not respond quickly. By the time the continuing education administrators at College A got internal approval to offer off-campus courses, College B had successfully established itself as the preeminent provider of off-campus courses. After two years of trying to establish itself in this market, College A stopped offering off-campus courses.

> A creative continuing education programmer at a liberal arts college in the West developed a proposal for a course on retirement planning for doctors. He reasoned that such a course was not available in the community, and the audience could afford to pay a high price. The idea was not imple-

mented, however, because the dean of continuing education realized that the college faced eventual competition from the continuing education division of the local medical school, which had a life-span integration approach to its program offerings. Although the dean believed his college could have initiated such a course successfully, he thought that as soon as the medical school saw what was happening, it would be likely to create a similar course. It had access to the same lists of doctors, and it had credibility with these doctors that the small college did not have. There was little question that in competition for the same market, the medical school would prevail.

Competitive Strategy

Competitive strategy is that combination of actions and policies which allows the provider to defend its position and to prosper in an increasingly competitive environment. There are many different ways to achieve prosperity; there is no single *best* competitive strategy. Different providers may coexist in the same market precisely because each has defined a particular strategy that has certain appeals to certain learners and allows the provider to avoid direct competition with any other provider. The best strategy for a given provider is almost always unique, tailored to its individual background and circumstances.

There are, nonetheless, two basic requirements for any competitive strategy. The first is that it reflect changes in the external environment. No strategy will succeed for long if it ignores educational, demographic, economic, or social trends. The second requirement is that the strategy be internally consistent. The different strategic variables must fit together in a coherent, mutually supportive way. Thus, for example, one would expect a provider with a high risk-orientation also to have relatively high financial flexibility and a supportive relationship with its parent organization. A provider whose policy is to price its programs above the going market rates can usually do so because it specializes, maintains a high-quality image, or is a technological leader. Another provider, competing with low prices, may support that strategy with low operating costs and no ancillary services. Whatever strategy is followed, the key operating policies must reinforce one another.

Porter (1980) suggests that there are three *generic* strategies, each of which is internally consistent, and each of which should allow a provider to create a position that can be maintained in the long term and that will lead to better-than-average results. These three strategies are: overall cost leadership, differentiation, and focus. Effective implementation of any of these generic strategies requires that all members of the organization understand what the strategy is. In addition, organizational arrangements must support the basic strategy rather than work at cross-purposes to it. Each of the three generic strategies is discussed in turn below.

Overall Cost Leadership. The first strategy seeks to establish overall cost leadership among the providers in the community. Cost leadership can be achieved through a set of functional policies, rigorously adhered to and all aimed at this basic objective. Policies that support this strategy are: minimizing investment in office space; renting classroom space as needed rather than owning or leasing on a long-term basis; computerizing records and information processing as much as possible to reduce payroll costs; offering a single, coherent set of programs that can be marketed together rather than diversifying and requiring several different marketing approaches for different audiences; concentrating advertising in one or possibly two heavily used media rather than using several different media; hiring faculty only as needed; cutting any course or program that does not meet predetermined financial goals; and offering only those ancillary services that the targeted learners absolutely need.

Implemented together, these policies can give a provider a significant cost advantage over other providers. That cost advantage can be used in one of two ways. If the provider keeps prices at the same level as other providers, the cost advantage may produce above-average profits. Alternatively, the provider can use the cost advantage to reduce prices below what others are charging, use this price differential to attract clients, and thereby increase market share.

There are typically one or two providers in every large metropolitan area who follow a cost leadership strategy. They are not university based, nor are they connected with a long-established cultural institution. They are free-standing adult education programs; in many cases they offer recreational courses to a young, professional audience.

Why is the cost leadership strategy not used more widely? There are several explanations. First, the prices charged to consumers of continuing education throughout the community are not high. In order to attract learners, especially in a competitive environment, most providers already keep their prices as low as practicable. As a result, there is not a high price-standard against which a low-cost provider's prices appear significantly lower.

Second, because price is so infrequently used as a marketing tool in continuing education, adult learners—the consumers of continuing education—are not accustomed to choosing courses or programs on the basis of price. The adult learner population is extraordinarily diverse. Some choose courses on the basis of location, others on the basis of a provider's reputation, and still others on the basis of ancillary services. The number of learners who do, or who would, select a continuing education program primarily on the basis of price is currently only a small fraction of the total market. So the notion of using a cost leadership strategy as a way of significantly increasing market share does not correspond to the present-day realities of the continuing education field.

This is not to say that the cost leadership strategy should be ignored, however. As continuing education becomes increasingly ingrained in the national consciousness as an integral part of personal and career development, the number of recurrent (as opposed to first-time) learners will increase. In business terminology, the market will "mature," and it will become possible to segment the audience of learners in new ways. Eventually, an existing or a new provider, using a cost leadership strategy, may well be able to promote its programs on the basis of "same quality, lower prices." If such a theme is used repeatedly and if quality is indeed comparable, it may be possible to uncover a sizable market segment that will choose continuing education offerings primarily on the basis of price. In the hands of creative, entrepreneurial providers, cost leadership could represent a significant strategic opportunity in continuing education.

Differentiation. The second generic strategy seeks to distinguish the provider from all other providers in the community. With this strategy, the provider seeks to establish and maintain a unique image or reputation. Advertising and other marketing efforts are used consistently to underscore the name and the special character of the provider.

There are several ways to differentiate. One is to emphasize the name and reputation of the parent institution. Harvard's extension program and the Smithsonian Institution's Resident Associate Program are two examples of providers that do this successfully. Much of their appeal to learners lies not in their specific course offerings (even though these are of high quality) but rather in the parent institution's own desirable attributes. Differentiation along these lines is easy to describe but difficult to implement, especially for a recent entrant into the field of continuing education, unless there is already a prestigious parent institution whose name carries weight in the community.

In the absence of a long tradition in the community or an established reputation for excellence, a provider can differentiate on the basis of other attributes. One provider may style itself a place for fun and social opportunities. Another may advertise all its programs as up-to-the-minute or state-of-the-art. Another offers programs for aspiring business leaders. Yet another may invest in the latest technology and emphasize technological leadership. Providers can also differentiate on the basis of services. Much of the appeal of community colleges, for example, lies in the counseling, academic support, and other services they provide.

In some cases, a provider wanting to pursue a differentiation strategy need only identify those attributes that already set it apart—for example, an unusually attractive location—and then emphasize them consistently in a coordinated marketing campaign. In other cases, the differentiating qualities are not obvious, or they do not yet exist. In these instances, a provider may be able to establish some distinguishing characteristic, such as those mentioned above. Such an approach demands that all internal functional policies be coordinated in support of the differentiation strategy.

The goal of differentiating is to attract students to the provider as an institution rather than to sell specific programs to specific clienteles. The strongest indication that a differentiation strategy is successful comes when learners say, "I think I'll see what _____ is offering this semester."

A successful differentiation strategy depends upon a sustained, consistent marketing effort to establish the provider's unique image. It also depends, of course, on constant monitoring of the program offerings to ensure that they live up to the public perception being encouraged. When differentiation is successful, it creates something of a shield against competition. Enrollees feel a sense of loyalty or membership; they share in the image, the prestige, the distinctiveness of the provider; thus they are less likely to be attracted to another provider. Learners may also tolerate slightly higher prices because of the prestige image of a provider.

Specialization or Focus. The final generic strategy involves intentionally restricting the scope of a provider's activities in order to focus on a particular group of learners, geographical region, or subject area. Since this is perhaps the best-known strategy in the field of continuing education, it is possible to cite many examples.

Some institutions were created to serve a specialized or focused continuing education market. From the day they opened their doors, community colleges have catered to the educational needs of their specific geographical communities. The Alliance Française has always specialized in the teaching of French. The American Institute for Banking was designed to serve the professional education needs of the banking community.

Other institutions were not originally providers of continuing education but have long since realized that they could extend their missions to continuing education through strategies of specialization. Most professional schools, for example, no longer limit themselves to pre-service training; they have become continuing education providers, and the strategy they follow is one of specialization in a targeted professional market. Many art museums have also specialized—in fine and applied arts and art appreciation courses—as a natural outgrowth of their original mission. Likewise, many hospitals have community education programs offering courses on health issues for people living in the hospital's service area.

A third group of providers is relatively new to continuing education and has decided that a specialization strategy offered the best opportunity to compete. One example comes from the Boston area, which is home to well over two hundred organizations offering continuing education. In the mid 1980s, Lasell Junior College chose to enter this crowded market by creating a program for women that concentrated on entry-level preparation for three career areas: fashion merchandising, travel and tourism, and electronic office management. In addition to its course work, Lasell focused all internships and placement efforts on these three specific fields.

The specialization strategy is based upon serving a particular target very well. It rests on the premise that the provider will be able to attract learners by serving its narrow strategic target more effectively than competitors with broader curricula and clienteles.

The advantages of specialization are many. If a provider specializes in a particular geographic area, as community colleges do, it is able to create information and service networks throughout that community. It discovers emerging needs in the community and reallocates resources to meet those needs. It can engage faculty for their skill in working with a local clientele rather than for their reputations as scholars. It becomes the first place that individuals, agencies, and businesses turn to when they need any kind of educational program, and this is a decided competitive advantage. A new provider will find it difficult to make inroads into this market because it does not enjoy the same mutually dependent relationship with the community as the existing provider.

If a provider specializes in a specific field of study (Russian, mental health, taxation, Jewish studies, music, or almost any imaginable subject), as long as there is a group of learners who value expertise in that subject, the provider will have a competitive advantage. For the provider can plausibly contend that it offers more breadth and depth in its chosen field than any other provider, and that its faculty represent the greatest expertise available locally.

One risk of the specialization strategy is that the field of specialization might be so broad that another provider could develop a subspecialty within it and attract some of the original provider's clientele. In one southern state, for example, a music school was serving all the music education needs of a community. It lost some of its students, however, to a new school that specialized in jazz. Later, it lost more of its students when a group of its faculty broke away to create a new school specializing in early music. A community college is vulnerable to the same risk. Within its service area a new provider could attract learners by specializing, for example, in technology-based vocational programs.

Providers who specialize must understand, too, that they will never reach a large market. Their strength lies in serving a particular market segment very well and thereby accepting a self-imposed limitation. To compensate for a smaller market, there are three financial benefits that can accrue to a provider who specializes. First, the provider may cultivate a large repeat clientele, each learner taking several courses over an extended period of time. The provider thereby enjoys a cost advantage over competitors who have to spend money to attract all new learners several times a year. Second, the provider may be able to charge higher prices for its programs because of its perceived expertise. Third, because the scope of its programs is limited either geographically or thematically, the provider should be able to find ways to cut costs—ways that are not available to providers serving a much broader population. For example, advertising can be limited to publications with targeted readerships, rather than high-cost, mass market media such as radio and newspaper.

"Stuck in the Middle" and Other Problems

Porter (1980) contends that a provider that fails to develop its strategy consistently in one of these three directions is in an extremely poor competitive position. Not having devoted its resources to establishing a viable long-term position, it is "stuck in the middle." At times, perhaps, it pursues a strategy of differentiation, trying to establish and sell a positive image of the organization as a whole. At other times, seeing opportunities to reach certain markets, it may adopt a specialization strategy. It thereby leaves itself open to strong competition from those who compete consistently on the basis of price or image or specialization. The provider that attempts to be all things to all people serves no one's needs especially well over the long run.

The lack of a single clear, well-implemented strategy in many cases reflects organizational confusion about such issues as mission and goals. ("Are we a professional school or are we a community service organization?" "First they tell me to generate a surplus, and then they tell me I have to use ineffective faculty." "The Board wants us to keep our old programming mix, but we have new competition that's stealing away half of our students.") Continuing education administrators get mixed messages about what they should do—and what they can do. Mandates coming from different quarters conflict with one another or with the realities of the marketplace. Organizational arrangements do not support a common strategy. When a provider is "stuck in the middle," it is usually because there is not a shared understanding of the provider's real strengths and weaknesses or a shared vision of whom the provider should be serving and how.

There are other threats to the implementation of a coherent strategy. One of the most common comes from the temptation to grow. In a competitive market, of course, the prospect of growth has particular appeal. When a provider is doing well with one coherent strategy, the temptation is to try to do more, to reach out in new directions, with different programs, to different clienteles. Such growth can succeed if it is a natural extension of the work the provider is already doing and if it builds upon existing organizational arrangements and staff competences. If, on the other hand, growth involves latching on to new topics in which the provider has no experience, no credibility, nor any cost advantage, the likelihood of sustained success is small. And short-term success that cannot be sustained may result in certain long-term costs. Faculty members may become disgruntled, students disappointed, and the provider's public image—at best—muddled.

If these mistakes are to be avoided, a provider needs to think clearly about its long-term interests and capabilities. Senior administrators must become participants in a thoughtful discussion. (The increasing competitiveness of the continuing education field provides a natural impetus for such a discussion.) A clear sense of priorities, of where and how the provider will—and will not—compete should emerge. In formulating a competitive strategy, the ultimate goal should be to identify that strategy which is best suited to the provider's strengths and which is least replicable by competitors.

References

Abell, D., and Hammond, J. S. *Strategic Market Planning: Problems and Analytical Approaches.* Englewood Cliffs, N.J.: Prentice-Hall, 1979.

Andrews, K. *The Concept of Corporate Strategy.* Homewood, Ill.: R. D. Irwin, 1980.

Christensen, C. R., Andrews, K. R., and Bower, J. L. *Business Policy: Text and Cases.* Homewood, Ill.: R. D. Irwin, 1978.

Drucker, P. F. *Management: Tasks, Responsibilities, Practices.* New York: Harper & Row, 1974.

Kotler, P. *Marketing for Non-Profit Organizations.* Englewood Cliffs, N.J.: Prentice-Hall, 1982.

Kotler, P., and Fox, K.F.A. *Strategic Marketing for Educational Institutions.* Englewood Cliffs, N.J.: Prentice-Hall, 1985.

Lovelock, C. H. *Services Marketing: Text, Cases, and Readings.* Englewood Cliffs, N.J.: Prentice-Hall, 1984.

Lovelock, C. H., and Weinberg, C. B. *Marketing for Public and Nonprofit Managers.* New York: Wiley, 1984.

Merson, J. C., and Qualls, R. L. *Strategic Planning for Colleges and Universities: A Systems Approach to Planning and Resource Allocation.* San Antonio, Tex.: Trinity University Press, 1979.

Newman, W. H., Logan, J. P., and Hegarty, W. H. *Strategy, Policy, and Central Management.* Cincinnati, Ohio: South-Western Publishing, 1985.

Porter, M. E. *Competitive Strategy.* New York: Free Press, 1980.

Porter, M. E. *Competitive Advantage: Creating and Sustaining Superior Performance.* New York: Free Press, 1985.

Shanklin, W. L., and Ryans, J. R. *Thinking Strategically: Planning for Your Company's Future.* New York: Random House, 1985.

Clifford Baden is director of Programs in Professional Education at the Harvard Graduate School of Education and director of Harvard's Institute for the Management of Lifelong Education.

A successful strategy considers the characteristics and constraints of the continuing education field.

Competitive Strategy in a Fragmented Field

Clifford Baden

Selection of a competitive strategy will be influenced in large measure by one's understanding of the field within which one is competing. Every field or industry or profession has certain defining characteristics. These are suggested in such questions as the following:

1. What is the nature of the relationship between providers and clients? Are there few providers for many clients? Are there many providers for few clients? How easy is it for clients to switch from one provider to another?

2. Do most clients conform to a standard consumption pattern or profile? Do they typically want the same goods or services in the same sequence? Or are their needs more diverse? Or are they unpredictable?

3. How do providers typically relate to one another? Do they compete, or do they collaborate? Do they ignore each other or are they indifferent?

4. Over time, do most providers tend to look and behave like one another?

5. How important is tradition as an explanation of behavior in the field? Are operating policies the way they are because they have to be or simply because "they've always been that way"? How susceptible is the field to innovation?

For each continuing education provider, the choice of a strategy of course depends on the provider's internal strengths and resources (described in Chapter One). But in order to succeed, a strategy must also recognize the parameters and constraints of the continuing education field itself, as suggested by the questions above. Providers need to understand why the field behaves the way it does, what truths about the field the most successful providers have understood and capitalized on, and where the opportunities for change are.

In this chapter we discuss continuing education as a *fragmented* field. The term comes from Porter's work (1980) on industry analysis. Porter defines a *fragmented industry* as one "in which no firm has a significant market share and can strongly influence the industry outcome" (p. 191). The continuing education field is in an analogous position. It, too, can be described as fragmented. There is no single market leader with the power to shape events for all other providers. Even a group of four or five large national providers that establish curricula or price policies for all others to follow is nowhere in evidence. Instead, a very large number of small-scale providers coexist in continuing education. Most of them serve a limited geographical market, and each has a very small share of the total market. Why is this so? What are the factors that make continuing education a fragmented field?

Why Is the Field Fragmented?

The most fundamental reason for fragmentation in continuing education is that there are virtually no barriers to entry into the field. Almost anyone or any organization can become a provider (and there are times when it seems that this has indeed happened!). Churches, community centers, YMCAs, freelance consultants, professional associations, hospitals, businesses, libraries—there are few organizations in this country that have not mounted courses, seminars, or conferences either for their own members or for the community at large. And virtually every school system, college, and university has become a provider of continuing education. No self-respecting school would limit its services to its traditional clientele now, when there are so many thousands of adults in the community to be served under an expanded notion of institutional mission.

Ease of entry into the field can be explained by several factors. These are discussed briefly below.

Low Entry Costs. In the automobile industry, tens of millions of dollars of investment are necessary before the first car can be manufactured. In any small retail operation, thousands of dollars of inventory must be purchased before the doors are opened for business. In contrast, no large investments are necessary in order to become a continuing education provider. The costs of starting a program are virtually nil. High technology is not characteristic of the field. There are no inventory costs. The prevailing paradigm is still that of a teacher spending time with a group of students.

What does it take for an individual to become a provider for the first time? With a small display advertisement in the local paper or some notices pasted on telephone poles and bulletin boards, anyone can offer a course. Organizations can get into the field just as easily. (Consider the number of college alumni associations that have begun programming for their members.) A course or even a series of courses can be developed entirely on speculation. If too few people enroll and the courses must be canceled, there are almost no out-of-pocket costs. With so little financial risk attached to entry, it is no surprise that so many are willing to try it.

No Advantages to Size. Economies of scale might serve to keep potential entrants out of the field because they would find it too expensive to start competing, in a cost-effective way, with existing providers. But it is difficult to name many instances of economies of scale in continuing education. True, a large university program, for example, can spread its administrative costs over many programs—but this has not deterred a host of new providers from entering the field. They may have noticed that administration tends to expand in proportion to the number of courses offered or students served, so the large provider does not really enjoy significant economies of scale.

New providers may also have recognized that it is not imperative to be large in continuing education in order to be credible. In the public imagination, the quality of a learning experience is not correlated with the size of the provider. "Boutique" operations can thrive in a competitive marketplace by appealing to a clientele that values small scale. The need to attain a certain "critical mass" before beginning operations is *not* a factor in starting up new continuing education operations.

No Regulation. Entry of new providers into the continuing education field is easy also because the field is unregulated. In other fields, where government standards for licensure or accreditation of providers exist, those standards commonly have the effect of limiting the total number of providers. No such standards exist in noncredit continuing education. Anyone can become a provider without first having to demonstrate either fiscal solvency or faculty qualifications. And many would argue that the crazy-quilt pattern of diversity that results—from the immense to the tiny operation, from the highly academic to the frivolous—is appropriate and desirable in continuing education. Regulation makes sense for credit-bearing or credentialing programs. But for noncredit or recreational programs, control and uniformity seem less suitable than choice and diversity.

Little Loyalty to Providers. If, having enrolled once with a provider, the typical learner thereafter remained loyal to that provider, such loyalty would constitute a potential barrier for new providers. They would be less willing to enter the field because they would need to spend more (on advertising, on added services, and so on) to woo learners away from their current providers. But learners do not remain loyal, because their interests and needs change over time. Most participation in continuing education is discretionary rather than mandatory, and the ability to choose what is of greatest appeal at the moment is one of continuing education's attractions to learners. In situations where learners have choices, learner loyalty in continuing education is notoriously low.

Easy Access to Learners. If learners could be approached only through their employers, for example, providers would engage in intense competition with one another (on the basis of price or of the spectrum of courses offered) in order to secure contracts with employers. After a while, the field would be reduced to a small number of large, powerful providers. But this is not the way the field works. Adults can be reached in any one of a dozen different environments—home, work, church, public transportation, retail stores, and so on. They can also be reached through many different media—radio, newspapers, direct mail, word-of-mouth, and so on. Entry into the continuing education field is made easy by the fact that access to learners is so easy. No provider or group of providers so monopolizes a large number of learners as to exclude other providers from entering the field.

These five factors explain why there are so many providers competing for a share of the continuing education market. But why does each of these providers serve only a geographically limited market? Why is competition typically thought of at the local rather than the national level in continuing education? This phenomenon of many providers with small, local market shares is a defining characteristic of a fragmented field. It is typical of service industries generally and can be explained by several factors.

Geographical Limitations. Given the prevailing model of a teacher working with a group of students, there are limits to the geographical area that any provider can service economically. Perhaps the learners come to the provider's establishment; perhaps the provider sends instructors to community sites. In either case, the delivery of services depends upon some movement of people, and this restricts the region a provider can serve from a single base of operations.

Diverse Learner Needs. A national provider of continuing education might emerge if it were possible to identify a standardized formula for program offerings that could appeal to tens of thousands of learners across the country. But consider the variables in the continuing education marketing mix: course topic, academic rigor, opportunities for socializing, price, location, meeting schedule, provider reputation, instructor qualifications, counseling services, and other ancillary services. There are dozens of permutations of these variables—and groups of learners interested in almost any possible combination. The field is fragmented in large part because learners' needs are so fragmented. A standardized model of continuing education has never been advanced as an ideal. Adult learners in particular expect their individual interests to be recognized and catered to. Thus, demand for any particular type of course or program is often relatively small. As a result, there probably is not enough volume to support production or marketing strategies that would yield an advantage to the larger national provider.

Importance of Local Standing. Many providers believe that an important ingredient in their success is the strong local ties they have established. They have a local reputation for quality. Their instructors come from and are known to the local community. These providers work with local businesses and agencies to develop, market, and deliver new programs that meet community needs. When local image and local contacts are key success factors, a field will be fragmented. Large national or even regional providers will not be able to compete successfully where they lack the strategic advantages of the smaller, local provider.

Diversity of Provider Goals. A final explanation for the fragmentation of the continuing education field is that different providers come to the field with very different orientations and goals. Contrast this with the private corporate sector, where profitability is the common orientation and measure of success. Profitable firms remain in an industry and grow; the unprofitable soon cease to compete. In continuing education, however, orientations may be very different. Some providers that do not care at all about market share or profitability stay in the field in order to serve their mission long after they have ceased to be viable competitors from any economic perspective. For example, the dean of one professional school insisted that a certain local clientele be served by the school's faculty, even though there was no way to do so without incurring a loss. Meanwhile, the same clientele was being served by other providers, including some for whom financial considerations were irrelevant and others for whom profitability was imperative.

In the continuing education field, there is no clearing mechanism, such as the profitability criterion, that serves to eliminate inefficient performers from the field. Inefficient providers operate alongside efficient providers and limit the ability of the latter to increase their market share. The ability of many different providers to coexist, each with different orientations and goals, adds to the fragmentation of the field.

Competing in a Fragmented Field

We have identified nine factors that contribute to the fragmentation of the continuing education field in this country: low entry costs, no advantage of size, lack of regulation, little loyalty to providers, easy access to learners, geographical limitations, diverse learner needs, the importance of local standing, and diversity of providers' backgrounds and goals. Most observers (and most providers) would accept these as characteristic of the continuing education field today. All of these factors help to explain a field in which one finds a great number of small-scale competitors, none of which is able to capture a large share of the market. Such fragmentation could be a prescription for cutthroat competition, leading at best to marginal profitability for all. In fact, however, many continuing education providers are thriving in this environment. They understand the root causes of fragmentation in the field; they have learned to cope with it; and they have achieved great success even though they capture only a small share of the total market.

For the continuing education provider that wants to compete successfully, there are a number of strategies for dealing with the fragmentation in the field. Essentially, these are specific adaptations of the generic strategies described in Chapter One. They are effective ways to exploit the provider's resources in the complex competitive environment of this field.

Specialize by Course Topic or Type. If learners' needs are so diverse that it is impossible to serve them all, specialization becomes an attractive option. Successful examples of this strategy abound. Providers concentrating in business and management topics are well established in most large communities. Specialists in computer training are a more recent example. In many cities, new providers are specializing in "urban life-style" courses: wine tasting, art collecting, visits with local chefs, and so on. Language schools, art schools, and music schools have prospered for many years by specializing.

The specialization strategy recognizes that size is not a necessary key to success in continuing education; small, well-managed programs can and do thrive. But because the strategy allows the provider to become especially well informed about a limited subject matter and to manage its resources in support of a single, well-defined objective, credibility results that can lead to growth. The provider can expand its course offerings or add ancillary services related to its area of expertise. The community is likely to respond when the specialist provider sends out course bulletins noting that certain new topics are particularly worthy of attention. The provider that follows a specialization strategy is more likely than others to succeed in promoting a special lecture program, a new series of publications, or a study tour related to its area of expertise.

Focus on Geographical Area. Even though a significant market share is out of reach and there are no national economies of scale, there may be substantial economies in blanketing a limited geographical area. Providers who follow this strategy concentrate their facilities and marketing attention on a single locale. This strategy economizes on the use of direct mail and advertising dollars, eliminates duplication of resources, and produces a better match of supply and demand in course offerings. Having operations spread out across a wide geographical area, in contrast, accentuates the difficulties of competing in a fragmented field.

Decentralize. Nonetheless, there are some providers that—by choice or by mandate—operate in more than one location. They are successful because they recognize an important characteristic of the field: the need for close personal attention and a local management orientation. They build this into their strategy rather than trying to work around it. They do not attempt to centralize all decisions at one location. Instead, they work deliberately to keep individual operations as small and autonomous as possible. Some state college systems with many campuses operate in just this way. Some of the newer noncredit franchise organizations follow a similar strategy, allowing each local operation as much autonomy as possible to accommodate the particular character of the host community.

Add Distinctive Features. Many providers offer courses similar to those offered elsewhere in the community. Course descriptions are approximately the same, and there is little price differential. In such cases, an effective strategy may be to increase the appeal of course offerings by providing ancillary services that learners want. Continuing education providers that have built new conference facilities or executive education centers in the last ten years are following such a strategy. They are differentiating themselves not on the basis of course offerings or even of institutional reputation but rather on the basis of desirable ancillary services. Some continuing education programs that find themselves in a competitive market differentiate themselves by offering wine and cheese parties periodically for their students. They have understood that socializing is an important consideration in course selection for a segment of the learner population.

Overcoming Fragmentation

Most successful providers today recognize the causes of fragmentation in this field and have adopted a strategy that acknowledges that fragmentation. They prosper in a limited market and accept their limited market share as an inevitable condition of operating in a highly diversified field.

There is a second, more provocative way to think about fragmentation. That is to ask, What are the possibilities of overcoming fragmentation? What if fragmentation were not inevitable but merely representative of the current state of development in continuing education? The future of continuing education may well belong to those providers who do *not* accept fragmentation as inevitable. Providers who can find a way to overcome barriers to size and to increased market share will enjoy significant strategic opportunities. It is possible to imagine some interesting scenarios that could change the structure of the field. And in some cases, providers are already pointing in new directions.

Creating Economies of Scale. Economies of scale exist when the provider's per-unit costs go down because it is able to reach large numbers of learners within a given time period. Economies of scale not only give the provider a cost advantage but also reduce exposure to competition because other providers cannot compete on an equal footing without first having reached the same size. We have said that economies of scale are not characteristic of the continuing education market, and that is historically true. But technological changes often create opportunities for economies of scale.

Technology can lead to economies of scale in delivery systems. It offers opportunities to overcome the limitations of the traditional ratio of one teacher to twenty students. Examples go back at least as far as the 1950s, when "Sunrise Semester" offered college-credit courses on television to residents of the greater New York City area. Videocassettes are a current example of a widespread, readily accessible technology offering new delivery options. The Massachusetts Institute of Technology, for example, videotapes its graduate-level courses and sells them on a subscription basis to practicing engineers around the country. On a more sophisticated level are interactive videodiscs. And there are still untapped possibilities in computer networking, teleconferencing, and satellite transmission. The National Technological University is another instance of technology's creating economies of scale. It comprises twenty-two universities joined together to provide high-technology continuing education throughout the country via telecommunications. If this experiment succeeds, it has the potential to draw learners away from smaller, local providers of similar courses because local providers cannot compete with the wealth of teaching resources available over the national network.

The airplane represents another example of technology's making possible new economies of scale in continuing education delivery systems. Some providers organize an intensive one-day or two-day program and offer it at various sites around the country. A single direct mail piece is used to announce offerings at multiple sites. The instructor travels by air to locations with high concentrations of learners. Within the continuing education field itself there are several providers who have used this strategy successfully: individuals such as Anver Suleiman and Ralph Elliot, and organizations such as the Learning Resources Network and the College Board's Office of Adult Learning Services. It remains to be seen whether telecommunications will affect the strategy of these providers.

Economies of scale can exist not only in the production and delivery of courses but also in marketing. National network television has not yet been used to advertise continuing education, but it is possible to imagine instances in which it might be. The American Association of Community and Junior Colleges, for example, could mount a credible national campaign on behalf of the vocational learning opportunities at the country's community and junior colleges.

Neutralizing Fragmentation. For many adults, personal teacher-learner contact is an important and desirable aspect of continuing education. We have said that this is one factor that explains the fragmentation of the field. Some providers have viewed it differently. Rather than allow the need for teacher-learner contact to lead to fragmentation and low market share, they have separated the activity of teaching from other aspects of the continuing education enterprise in order to enjoy the advantages of greater market share. Two examples illustrate this strategy:

> Elderhostel is a successful nationwide program of course offerings for older adults. Courses at college campuses around the country are announced in a catalogue mailed from the program's Boston office. Participants register and pay through this single office, then travel to the college they have selected, where they study for a week or more. The scope of the program has grown from regional to national to international and has expanded from its initial focus on summer courses to year-round programming.

Elderhostel has successfully overcome fragmentation in two ways. First, of course, it recognized that—despite the presumed fragmentation of the learner population—there is a very large (and growing) category of learners with common characteristics: older adults with free time and some disposable income, a liking for travel, and the desire to learn. Second, organizationally, Elderhostel separated administration (that is, marketing and registration) from the actual delivery of courses. It left in place the personalized, localized teacher-learner contact that learners wanted. But it took some of the invisible administrative functions and centralized them in a national office.

The range of course offerings in the Elderhostel catalogue surpasses anything that a local provider could possibly offer. As a result, Elderhostel has become a widely recognized standard in programming for older adults. Other providers who want to reach this same audience must take pains to distinguish themselves from this program. Are there other identifiable market segments for which a similar national strategy could be implemented?

> Thomas A. Edison State College in New Jersey does not offer courses. Instead, it evaluates students' prior learning, helps them to select appropriate learning experiences that

can lead to degree completion, and awards degrees. It serves students far beyond its local geographical area, and its growth potential is great. It has overcome fragmentation by uncoupling the awarding of credit from the delivery of courses.

These two strategies acknowledge the need for teacher-learner contact and the need for individualized course selection—both of which are traditionally fragmenting conditions. But the two providers just discussed have identified other aspects of the continuing education enterprise that are subject to consolidation, which allows an increase in market share.

It is possible to imagine professional associations or labor or industry groups following a similar strategy—that is, serving as national centers for marketing, registration, or accreditation of locally delivered courses. A push in this direction might come from two sources. The national organizations might encourage it in order to impose some standards on the field and to create some transportable, nationally recognized credentials. Providers might also welcome the opportunity to become the locally accredited source of learning, particularly if they thought they could get an exclusive local franchise and thereby gain a competitive advantage in the local market.

Summary

The continuing education field has traditionally been fragmented. This fact can be explained by several underlying characteristics of the field. Those providers who have prospered have recognized the causes of fragmentation and have adopted strategies that tacitly acknowledge those causes.

A few innovative providers have looked at the same characteristics and decided that they are not inevitable or immutable but simply representative of traditional ways of operating. These providers do not deny or ignore all the traditional causes of fragmentation. Rather, they focus on one or two barriers to consolidation and size and ask whether there are opportunities to overcome these barriers, while still serving learners' needs. Some innovators have taken advantage of technology to surmount certain barriers to size. Other innovators have thought of the continuing education enterprise as a series of discrete functions, some of which must be local and some of which can be centralized for greater efficiency.

The possibilities for rethinking the fragmentation of the field have hardly been exhausted. The next ten years are likely to see the emergence of many new strategies for competing—strategies that do not accept small market share as an inevitable corollary of being a provider of continuing education.

Reference

Porter, M. E. *Competitive Strategy.* New York: Free Press, 1980.

Clifford Baden is director of Programs in Professional Education at the Harvard Graduate School of Education and director of Harvard's Institute for the Management of Lifelong Education.

Large conglomerate providers enjoy certain competitive advantages, but they must plan carefully to retain them.

Strategic Market Planning in Conglomerate Continuing Education Programs

James P. Pappas

As I was completing the literature review for this chapter, mock-ups of the promotional materials for our spring advertising campaign were placed on my desk. Each quarter's campaign is built around a theme that tries to capture some underlying concept that characterizes the offerings. Past themes have included "Add a Little Class," "Aspire Higher," "Carried Away with Learning," and "Draw from Experience." The theme for spring, illustrated with various multicolored flowers, was "Discover the Diversity." The copywriter who had penned the theme line said she had been impressed by the wide variety and large number of courses, degrees, certificates, and conferences being offered.

Lying next to the mock-ups were two articles. One was titled "Strategies for Diversity" (Ansoff, 1957); the other (Berg, 1965) discussed diversification and size as the keys to success for conglomerate firms. It was interesting to note that the copywriter had so effectively identified the critical characteristics of a conglomerate continuing education provider.

This chapter will discuss the characteristics and advantages of such an organization and the strategies that can help it maintain a market leadership position.

Defining Conglomerate

What is a conglomerate? According to one management expert (Berg, 1965), "Conglomerate companies are typically 'large and diversified' . . . with at least five or six divisions . . . that sell different products to their own markets. . . . [T]hese various divisions typically function independently" (p. 79). Some continuing education providers are in an analogous position. They are large, as measured by revenues generated and number of students served. They are diversified, with credit and noncredit, on-campus and off-campus, day, evening, and weekend programs. They are organized into divisions, departments, or program areas, each of which functions relatively independently of the others. Examples of conglomerates include the continuing education divisions at schools such as the University of Minnesota, New York University, the University of California, Los Angeles, and the University of Utah.

As these examples imply, the continuing education conglomerate is typically attached to a "multiversity" that dominates the market by virtue of reputation or size. This is not to say that large universities automatically have conglomerate continuing education programs; in fact, many make the decision to limit, specialize, or decentralize their adult offerings. However, few small institutions have conglomerate continuing education programs, since they typically do not have the resources and facilities to support a large continuing education function.

Conglomerates control a large proportion of the local market and are perceived as market leaders in the positioning of their various programs (Berg, 1965; Kotler, 1984; Taylor, 1985). Additionally, most continuing education conglomerates are in markets with sufficient student populations to allow for considerable scope and diversity of programs. The larger the market, however, the greater the number of competing providers there are likely to be.

Advantages of Conglomerates

Economies of Scale. One of the most typical advantages of the conglomerate provider is that it has a larger market share and a larger funding base across which to spread its fixed operating expenses (Bloom and Kotler, 1975; Buzzell, Gale, and Sultan, 1975). Many of the expenses of providers of services such as continuing education are fixed for a specified number of units and then rise only slowly as additional units are added. For example, once a continuing education unit has established its registration and accounting offices, the incremental costs of serving another 1,000 or 2,000 students will be relatively small. The per-student cost of maintaining these functions decreases as the number of students increases—an economy of scale enjoyed by the conglomerate provider as compared to the smaller provider.

Economies of scale can also make a significant difference in promotional activities (Kotler, 1984; Taylor, 1985). Both small and large continuing education providers need promotional materials (a quarterly catalogue, direct mail fliers), but the unit costs are much lower when amortized over a large number of courses. For example, as the catalogue gets larger, the costs of producing additional pages with additional class descriptions become almost inconsequential.

Market Power. Many economists (Bain, 1968; Berg, 1965; Kotler, 1984), particularly those who study qualitative aspects of management (such as power, influence, strategy, and negotiation), suggest that direct economies of scale are less important than the marketplace power that a large and diversified organization can bring to bear. They argue that diversification and market share permit the economic entity to bargain more effectively in the marketplace. The conglomerate can, over the long run, administer prices in a way that will further control the market. The conglomerate continuing education provider is capable of absorbing losses temporarily in some of its courses in order to establish a favorable market presence and image. For example, one institution sponsored a prestigious summer arts festival through its continuing education division, even though the festival's earnings did not meet its expenses, in order to project an image of high quality. The losses were offset by enrolling a few more students in some large lecture classes (Psychology 101, Sociology 101), in which increased class size did not have a negative impact on students' perception of quality.

A conglomerate can also take advantage of its market position by slowly raising prices for a high-quality program (Ansoff, 1957; Evans, 1959; Kotler, 1984; Taylor, 1985; Wind, 1982). As a consequence, most conglomerates are able to move eventually into a prestige pricing format, which further increases their advantage because the return on investment is greater (Bloom and Kotler, 1975; Buzzell, Gale, and Sultan, 1975; Scheuble, 1964).

Quality of Administration. Many of these advantages overlap. When additional revenues are generated (either by profits or by a formula-driven, full-time equivalent funding base), they can be allocated to the hiring of better administrators and more creative programmers. Other things being equal, better personnel are attracted to conglomerate continuing education units that offer higher salaries or have better reputations. The diversity of programs of the conglomerate provider also offers greater potential for vertical or lateral career movement and job enrichment (Berg, 1965). Compared to the smaller provider, the conglomerate is more successful not only at attracting but also at retaining good employees.

Quality of Instruction. Correlatively, the conglomerate has a greater opportunity to attract superior teachers and trainers. The conglomerate, being typically part of a larger institution, has a larger pool of internal instructors to solicit for either overload or normal load teaching. If one can select a humanities instructor from the 200 to 300 faculty members and teaching assistants in the college of humanities, the likelihood of picking a particularly able instructor is far greater than it is for the smaller continuing education provider that has to hire someone from an internal pool of ten to twelve humanities professors. Because of the diversity of classes offered, the conglomerate programmer can also seek instructors with more specialized expertise to teach specialized courses, which, in turn, enhance the perception of responsiveness and quality. Conversely, the conglomerate programmer can identify the strong instructor who enjoys teaching continuing education classes and can offer him or her numerous teaching opportunities.

Finally, the continuing education conglomerate that has successfully projected a prestigious image is more attractive to the better instructors in the community. As these advantages accrue to the conglomerate, they ensure that it offers a higher quality of instructional product to its consumer group, which in turn increases its attractiveness to both internal and external constituents.

Bandwagon and Integration Effects. Leading manufacturers of consumer products enjoy a bandwagon effect for similar brand or company products: The satisfied owner of a Chrysler New Yorker is likely to buy a Plymouth Colt for his college-age daughter, and the soft drink consumer consistently chooses among numerous Coca-Cola products. So too for the conglomerate continuing education provider (Ansoff, 1957; Kotler, 1980; Taylor, 1985): The existence of quality programs in one area enhances the perceived quality of other programs. The social worker who takes an advanced psychotherapy course to meet mandated relicensure requirements and is satisfied is more likely to think of taking a leisure class in racquetball from the same continuing education conglomerate.

The bandwagon effect can also occur internally when one division programmer is inspired to create new courses or activities by developments in another division. A training program for using microcomputers in business, for example, can easily be modified to create a similar program in educational administration.

Because the conglomerate provider can offer many different subjects in many different formats, it can also take advantage of integration. (In business this concept is specified as "backward" or "forward" integration—extending the product line with new products that lead naturally to or from the original products.) Thus, for example, a popular advanced course on the history of Nazi Germany can lead to a new series of prerequisite courses or to a specialized master's degree program in World War II history that will attract some of the same audience. A conference or lecture series may suggest opportunities to create a new course. At one university, a successful course in landscape architecture led eventually to the creation of a home landscaping certificate program. Opportunities for this kind of integration are greater in continuing education conglomerates, where the structures for different programming options are already in place.

Product Development. Having a larger number of courses and a more diversified set of offerings allows the administrator of the continuing education conglomerate to absorb occasional losses in order to enhance product development over the long term. For example, the conglomerate can work with a weak course or instructor until the course content or the instructor's skills improve. The same opportunity typically will not be available to the smaller, specialized continuing education provider, which cannot afford financial losses, low enrollments, or a course likely to hurt the provider's image. Its size advantage allows the conglomerate to improve its product line through constant course development, upgrading, and refinement (Berg, 1965; Scheuble, 1964; Kotler, 1980).

Even more directly, as the conglomerate becomes larger and generates more resources, it can afford to pay for course development as well as instruction. For example, the small correspondence program may only be able to offer a single fee to an instructor to develop and grade a distance class. In the larger, adequately financed correspondence unit, which has the capacity to absorb development costs, the administrator can pay a prestigious faculty member to create the correspondence syllabus, texts, tests, and so on, and still have funds to hire a second instructor to do the grading. In addition to having higher-quality courses, the continuing education conglomerate enjoys two secondary benefits of its ability to utilize the services of senior faculty. Externally, it can promote its courses as being equivalent to regular courses. Internally, it can defuse political attacks on its programs by other university personnel who may take a dim view of continuing education.

Pricing of Infrequently Purchased Services. The above conditions provide a special advantage to the conglomerate, given the type of marketplace that exists in continuing education. Most nontraditional students take a class only infrequently and typically perceive it as expensive. If one adds the students' time and inconvenience to the cost, even low-tuition classes are expensive. Data from other types of business suggest that with infrequently purchased, high-priced items, consumers are more willing to pay a premium for what they perceive as quality (Kotler, 1980; Taylor, 1985). This is particularly true for services or products that are difficult for buyers to evaluate. As a result, the issues of quality and image, mentioned above, are critical for students who may not be very knowledgeable about shopping for continuing education classes. They solve their dilemma by simply buying more classes from the prestigious conglomerate (which retains their loyalty by pursuing a differentiation strategy, as described in Chapter One).

A related issue is that the education market is typically fragmented—that is, no single group of consumers accounts for a significant proportion of total sales. Since students are not concentrated in this way, they do not have the power to bargain for lower course prices. Students who feel they must buy from a prestigious provider to have some assurance of quality are unlikely to band together to bargain for better tuition rates. Thus, the conglomerate, with its larger share of a fragmented market, should be better able than smaller, less prestigious providers to manage the per-unit fees and realize higher profits.

There are, of course, some exceptions. The large engineering firm that buys a packaged, on-site master's program for its senior staff may very well negotiate at least partly on the basis of price. But such contract programs are just one part of the large and complex program mix that strengthens the conglomerate continuing education provider. The typical pattern of infrequent purchases and fragmented markets again accrues to the advantage of the conglomerate.

In reflecting on these various advantages, one starts to understand better why the conglomerate continuing education provider tends to become increasingly successful and profitable and to have high enrollments. As the dominant conglomerate continues to prosper through the advantages of size, it becomes more and more impervious to direct competition. This is so because of the very heavy investments that would be necessary for a significant competitor to emerge once the conglomerate is established in a particular market. Given the political climate, resources, and attitudes in most institutions, the costs of moving from a specialized market niche to full-scale conglomerate status would be prohibitive.

The smaller continuing education provider is therefore more successful with a well-focused market niche strategy. It can compete for a single, targeted group of learners, but it can only partially erode the conglomerate's strong market share position. The fact that conglomerates of all types enjoy significant advantages has been well documented by the Marketing Science Institute in their Profit Impact Market Strategies (PIMS) project (Schoeffler, Buzzell, and Heany, 1974; Buzzell, Gale, and Sultan, 1975). They tried to identify and measure major determinants of return on investment for business. Their empirically derived data base suggests that, on the average, a difference of 10 percentage points in market share is typically accompanied by a difference of 5 points in return on investment.

Additional research reported by James Taylor (1985) suggests that these same advantages accrue to diversified service conglomerates. If this is the case in educational settings as well, then the large continuing education conglomerate often enjoys an almost two-to-one tuition profit or enrollment advantage over the smaller, more focused provider. All this (and little likelihood of anti-trust action) should leave the conglomerate continuing education administrator happy.

However, as Ansoff (1957) has noted in his article on diversification, all is not sweetness and light for the conglomerate manager. Ansoff suggests that in the current marketplace this manager, like Wonderland's Red Queen, typically finds that "it takes all the running you can do to keep in the same place." While the advantages of the continuing education conglomerate make full-scale competition unlikely, many of its market segments are now being challenged.

Competitive Strategies for Conglomerates

Today's educational marketplace is increasingly competitive (Johnson, 1984; Pappas and Foster, 1983). If we add to the traditional institutions of post-secondary and higher education, which are constantly creating new programs to meet learners' needs, the newly emerging private providers of continuing education, public television telecourses, training by professional organizations, cultural enrichment and arts courses offered by museums and art centers, educational software for use with personal computers, and so on, we are confronted with the reality of a rapidly shifting marketplace. Even the dominant, diversified, highly reputed conglomerate will have to develop additional strategies to protect its advantages, profitability, or enrollments in certain segments.

As Kotler (1980) has suggested, any market strategy must take several factors into account. For continuing education providers these include (1) the unit's position in the market; (2) the unit's resources, objectives, and policies; (3) the competitors' marketing strategies; (4) the characteristics of the student audience; (5) the reputation and prestige of the institution; and (6) the character of the local economy. Given that these factors are part of any strategic thinking, how can the administrator capitalize on the particular advantages of the continuing education conglomerate in planning strategy? Seven approaches to thriving in a competitive marketplace are suggested below.

Fortification Through Pricing. Given all of its potential advantages, it is logical that the continuing education conglomerate should seek to retain its market leadership (Bloom and Kotler, 1975; Buzzell, Gale, and Sultan, 1975; Taylor, 1985). This may seem to be a simplistic assertion; however, central administrators at some institutions are suggesting that conglomerates should abandon an aggressive market leadership strategy in favor of a more focused, or limited, strategy. This may be a good suggestion for the market follower, for example, the third or fourth largest provider in the marketplace or a market-niche provider serving less than 5 percent of the potential market. However, the PIMS study mentioned above and recent supporting studies carried out by the Dover Corporation, Procter and Gamble, and McKinsey and Co. for the American Business

Conference (Kotler, 1980; Taylor, 1985) all suggest that conglomerate leadership is the very best position, and all market participants should aspire to it. One way to achieve this is through a strategy of fortification.

In a typical fortification strategy (Kotler, 1980; 1984), a dominant organization maintains its prices at a reasonable level in relation to the perceived value of its courses as compared to those of its competitors. This strategy, which can also be called a holding strategy, suggests that the conglomerate should not set its prices at the highest possible level. Instead, it should use its advantages to price its classes for protection and reasonable return. One rule of thumb consistently suggested in the literature is to price the product (the conglomerate's classes) at approximately 50 to 75 percent of the prevailing market price. Experience argues that the conglomerate's price should cover instructional and promotional costs, overhead, and a rate of return of approximately 8 to 10 percent. There should generally be some competitors in the market offering specialized programs that are more expensive, so that the consumer has a sense of value in approaching the conglomerate's courses; but the majority of offerings in the marketplace are priced at or below those of the conglomerate. Applying such a pricing strategy, the conglomerate can exploit its advantages of quality and breadth of offerings and still have a greater return on investment than its competitors.

Course and Program Innovation. To retain its market leadership, the continuing education conglomerate cannot rest on its laurels. It must innovate constantly. A conglomerate should use its advantages of high-quality staff and faculty, ability to spend more on development, ability to absorb losses, and leadership position to aggressively develop new courses and products. One university-based conglomerate, for example, developed two new master's programs in instrumentation physics and fuels technology after a survey showed that engineers in nearby computer and defense industries needed this type of specialized training. Both of these new products were modifications of existing engineering programs for these specific audiences. The conglomerate was able to price the products below those of a nearby engineering institute that could not amortize its administrative overhead and instructional costs across other institutional programs. Also, market followers could not create new programs quickly enough to compete. The continuing education unit demonstrated creativity on the part of programmers and faculty, and it reaffirmed in the eyes of the market its standing as a leader in product innovation.

For an innovation strategy to be successful, internal policies must encourage creativity and reward risk taking. There must be very few internal administrative barriers to the creation and implementation of new programs. Policy formulation and the development of intrainstitutional support for continuing education are a critical part of the administrator's role (Miller, 1981).

Emphasizing Quality. Most conglomerates should take an almost obsessive approach to achieving above-average quality in their courses and activities. Some of the additional revenues available to a conglomerate should be assigned to product evaluation (for example, course and faculty ratings and market surveys of past students) to ensure quality as high as or higher than that of competitors' products.

Because the conglomerate has a large number of courses, it can afford to reduce some of its weaker programs from time to time. The elimination of below-average instructors and classes on a regular basis should be a high-priority tactic for conglomerate administrators. While this task has to be approached with humaneness and sensitivity, the overriding concern must be to guarantee the student the best-quality education.

High quality is a goal that any parent organization is pleased to endorse. As mentioned above, the job of the continuing education conglomerate administrator is to have in place policies that give him or her the flexibility necessary to achieve this goal. Such policies include the right not to hire faculty from other campus units, the right to select qualified off-campus instructors, and enough discretion in setting salaries to hire first-rate programmers. The most uncomfortable position for the conglomerate administrator is being held accountable for a high-quality standard without having the flexibility necessary to achieve it.

Flanking and Extension Strategies. These concepts were discussed briefly in the earlier section on integration. They describe specific ways of extending the provider's product line to achieve greater market share. Both flanking and extension strategies take advantage of the conglomerate's size and diversity of program formats. Flanking seeks to take advantage of possible variations in times or sites of existing courses and programs. The project of Indiana/Purdue University Extension to move some of its campus courses to a shopping center site is a simple example of this. Many institutions package their regular degree programs in weekend configurations. This has proved particularly successful in executive business programs. A variation of this type of product flanking is to rearrange the curriculum to ensure that similar classes are offered on a consistent basis in the same time blocks. All parenting classes might be offered in the early evening on Tuesdays if a survey of homemakers indicates this to be the optimum time slot. Tuesday evenings would thus become established as continuing education times for this clientele. Another variation is to add a noncredit section to a credit class to attract students or auditors who would not enroll for credit. This is a particularly effective strategy if the institutional leadership can be convinced to charge adult auditors less than credit seekers.

Extension strategies involve the introduction of new products similar to current successful programs (Kotler, 1980; Lovelock and Weinberg, 1984). Again, this strategy takes advantage of the multiple program formats available to the conglomerate provider. A degree program may evolve from a series of popular courses, a degree program may generate a certificate program taking less time to complete, or a conference may grow out of a well-attended professional course. Successful examples of this include an evening certificate program in textiles developed after a series of art classes showed a strong market, a noncredit management certificate program that grew out of a well-received executive Master of Business Administration degree program, and a conference on the use of the polygraph inspired by a popular master's program in physiological psychology. For this strategy to succeed, the conglomerate administrator must encourage frequent sharing of information among the different program area heads. There must be structured incentives for such collaboration and disincentives for territoriality.

Providing Superior Service. One of the advantages that should accrue to a large conglomerate is that sufficient staff resources and staff training time ensure superior service to the student (Kotler, 1980; Lovelock and Weinberg, 1984). This may seem a bit anomalous, given the popular notion that in larger organizations the consumer typically receives little personal attention. Organizational personnel are expected to have minimal direct contact with any single client. However, superior customer service is a function of management attitude rather than organizational size. Dennis Johnson (1984), an educational marketing consultant, talks about the need to create in the continuing education unit a "Mickey Mouse" mentality. He suggests that Disneyland is among the better service providers in the country. Its attitudes about treating the customer as a guest and its continual indoctrination and training of staff provide a critical marketing edge for Disneyland as compared to its competitors. A conscious strategy on the part of a continuing education administrator to ensure that staff, faculty, and colleagues have such a service mentality is particularly important.

The large conglomerate can also assign some of its resources to specific learner-oriented services in ways that are not available to the smaller provider. A good example of this is the creation of specialized adult counseling centers in many conglomerates. These centers typically offer academic and career counseling, placement assistance, study skill programs, and day care services. The attention to individual needs that such services provide has a significant positive impact on the adult student.

Promotional Activities. In large corporations, one of the major strategies for maintaining market share has been heavy advertising and promotion (Ansoff, 1957; Berg, 1965; Kotler, 1980). This same strategy can be effectively used by the continuing education conglomerate (Pappas and Foster, 1983). However, it must be done with care: Political repercussions and consumer backlash can result if promotion is perceived as a misuse of educational funds (e.g., Miller, 1981). Almost all continuing education conglomerates are housed in post-secondary institutions, where colleagues—who probably see more public announcements of continuing education programs than of any other campus activity—become offended if the advertising is not done tastefully. In addition, legislators or trustees may react negatively if they judge heavy use of advertising inappropriate.

Even with these concerns, the continuing education unit should maintain a heavy schedule of promotional activities (approximately 8 to 10 percent of the budget after direct expenses). One approach to managing promotion in a subtle fashion is to send low-cost but graphically and textually high-quality brochures to the homes of potential students on a regular basis, even though they may not be part of the target audience for the class or program being advertised. This confirms in the mind of the potential consumer the image of breadth and diversity. Distributing catalogues by direct mail or as newspaper inserts is another way to maintain a high-visibility campaign that will be seen as appropriate. Heavy use of public relations tactics in promotional activities—for example, public service announcements in major urban and suburban newspapers and radio announcements for new degrees and programs—is also important. Many continuing education marketing experts (Suleiman, 1982) argue against the use of billboards, television, and general radio advertising. However, these can be very powerful promotional vehicles for a market leader if they are done creatively and if they focus on the general image of the provider rather than on specific programs. As Falk (1986) has suggested, the University of Utah has been particularly effective in using billboards and television in this way. The university uses a limited theme message to simply remind potential students of the beginning of the quarter, rather than advertising particular classes. These options are obviously more readily available to conglomerates, who can afford such expensive, generic techniques, than they are to their smaller competitors.

One additional key advantage that the conglomerate has is its ability to hire proficient copywriters, graphic artists, or ad agencies as staff or consultants. They are critical in creating a high-quality image. The smaller organization typically will not have the resources to match the conglomerate in such promotional expenses.

Responding to Social Concerns. One of the most constructive ways that a conglomerate can enhance its image and its general market position is to offer selective programs that demonstrate its social consciousness and service character. From time to time, the continuing education organization should mount programs that may lose or break even financially to show that it is willing to address urgent concerns of its internal or external community. For example, a conglomerate might sponsor a conference on nuclear war bringing in several nationally known speakers, even though the fees for the conference will not meet costs. One university-based conglomerate organized a week-long seminar on the political and religious teachings of Martin Luther King around the Martin Luther King holiday and a national conference on nuclear disarmament. Both programs generated considerable positive media coverage and legitimately met the university's community service obligations.

Summary

In an increasingly competitive marketplace, the conglomerate continuing education provider has many potential advantages: economies of scale, market power, the ability to attract top-quality teachers and administrators, the ability to integrate programs from different areas, opportunities for new product development, and flexibility in setting prices to achieve maximum enrollments and financial gain.

But in order to capitalize on and retain these potential advantages, the conglomerate provider must be vigilant. It must be aware of its different internal constituencies, the needs of the community it serves, and the program offerings of its competitors. It must deliberately pursue strategies—which are unavailable to or difficult for the smaller provider—in order to maintain its market leadership position. These strategies include a fortification pricing strategy, course and program innovation, emphasis on high quality, flanking and extension, investments in service, broad promotional activities, and socially responsive programming.

References

Ansoff, H. I. "Strategies for Diversification." *Harvard Business Review*, 1957, *35* (5), 113-114.
Bain, J. S. *Industrial Organizations*. 2nd ed. New York: Wiley, 1968.
Berg, N. "Strategic Planning in Conglomerate Companies." *Harvard Business Review*, 1965, *43* (3), 79-92.
Bloom, P. N., and Kotler, P. "Strategies for High Marketshare Companies." *Harvard Business Review*, 1975, *53* (6), 63-72.
Buzzell, R. D., Gale, B. T., and Sultan, G. M. "Market Share—A Key to Profitability." *Harvard Business Review*, 1975, *53* (1), 97-106.
Evans, M. K. "Profit Planning." *Harvard Business Review*, 1959, *37* (4), 45-54.
Falk, C. F. "Promoting Continuing Education Programs." In H. Beder (ed.), *Marketing Continuing Education*. New Directions for Continuing Education, no. 31. San Francisco, Jossey-Bass, 1986.
Johnson, D. "Creating the Institutional Attitude for Promotion." Paper presented at the American College Test National Center for the Advancement of Educational Practices Conference, San Francisco, Calif., May 10, 1984.
Kotler, P. *Marketing Management*. 4th ed. Englewood Cliffs, N.J.: Prentice-Hall, 1980.
Kotler, P. *Marketing Management*. 5th ed. Englewood Cliffs, N.J.: Prentice-Hall, 1984.
Lovelock, C. H., and Weinberg, C. B. *Marketing for Public and Nonprofit Managers*. New York: Wiley, 1984.
Miller, P. A. "Strengthening the University Continuing Education Mission." In

J. C. Votruba (ed.), *Strengthening Internal Support for Continuing Education.* New Directions for Continuing Education, no. 9. San Francisco: Jossey-Bass, 1981.

Pappas, J. P., and Foster, K. *Promotional Techniques and Practices for Recruiting Adults.* Iowa City, Iowa: American College Test Publications, 1983.

Scheuble, P. A. "ROI for New-Product Planning." *Harvard Business Review,* 1964, *42* (6), 110–120.

Schoeffler, S., Buzzell, R. D., and Heany, D. F. "Impact of Strategic Planning on Profit Performance." *Harvard Business Review,* 1974, *52* (2), 137–145.

Suleiman, A. S. *Developing and Marketing Successful Seminars and Conferences.* New York: The Marketing Federation, 1982.

Taylor, J. W. *Competitive Marketing Strategies.* Radnor, Pa.: Chilton, 1985.

Wind, Y. J. *Product Policy: Concepts, Methods and Strategy.* Reading, Mass.: Addison-Wesley, 1982.

James P. Pappas is associate dean, Division of Continuing Education, and professor of educational psychology at the University of Utah.

Increased attention to continuing professional education has resulted in intensified competition among program providers and the necessity for establishing a competitive edge for program survival.

Competitive Strategy in Continuing Professional Education

John F. Azzaretto

Meeting the educational needs of professionals has become big business. Much is at stake in this educational sweepstakes, including power, prestige, and money. With increased demand for continuing professional education, often due to mandatory requirements (Phillips, 1987), providers of such programs have likewise proliferated. Universities, professional associations, employers, and independent suppliers are currently the major organizations that provide continuing education to professionals (Houle, 1980; Stern, 1983). Each has distinctive strengths and resources upon which to draw in serving the educational needs of professionals.

The result is a subtle and at times overt competition among various program providers. A primary reason for this competition is ease of entry into the continuing professional education market. In addition, educational programs are easily transferable and can be readily adopted by competitors.

Providers of educational programs to professionals are not unlike other service organizations, such as airlines or hotels, which must maintain a competitive edge in order to meet client needs and prosper among similar service providers. Thus, a provider of continuing professional education, like any other business venture, wants to:

- Meet the legitimate needs of its clientele
- Maximize its influence over the particular segment of the community it serves
- Accumulate sufficient resources to sustain its members and extend the service it delivers
- Earn the recognition that comes with providing quality service
- Secure a leadership position with the service it renders.

The aim of this chapter is to help the provider achieve these goals. The focus is on building a competitive foundation, evaluating the internal context and external market structure, and mapping a competitive strategy for continuing professional educators. If today's program provider is to remain viable, its managers must organize and structure their activities to assure a competitive position over the long term.

Context for Delivery

With the explosion of knowledge in the mid 1960s came the societal demand that professional practitioners maintain and improve their skills. Parallel to this development was the growth of and increased emphasis on formal continuing education programs. As a result, such programs are flourishing today in business, teaching, accounting, law, medicine, and many other professions. In some fields, attendance at continuing professional education programs is required in order to maintain a license to practice. In other professions, some state legislatures have mandated training for practitioners (for example, pharmacists and law enforcement personnel); and in still other cases, professional associations (for example, accounting and engineering) require that members participate in formal continuing education programs in order to retain membership. In all likelihood, this market will grow without limits as (1) more and more occupations professionalize, (2) individual professionals seek formal programs to maintain and improve their effectiveness, and (3) mandatory continuing education for various professions increases.

In the current educational marketplace, providers of continuing professional education are as varied as they are numerous. However, several key actors emerge in the professional continuum of pre-service education, practice, and training for continued competency. The major providers of continuing professional education are (1) higher education institutions, both professional schools and continuing education and extension units; (2) professional associations; (3) employers, often through their human resource development units; and (4) a host of consultants and independent providers (Houle, 1980; Stern, 1983).

Professional schools within a university teach the systematic knowledge that is the basis of professional competence. Equally important to the preparation of students for practice is the professional school's responsibility for the transfer of new knowledge based on current research efforts. Universities provide this new information not only to current students but also to practicing professionals through continuing education courses, seminars, and institutes. As the primary source of knowledge and skill development for most professional disciplines, higher education has assumed an expanded mission, offering practitioners learning opportunities throughout their careers.

Professional associations tend to sponsor continuing education activities directly related to practitioner competence and professional performance (Hohmann, 1983). One of the essential attributes of the professional role is autonomy, of self-regulation by the professionals with regard to the development and application of the body of knowledge in which they alone are expert. Increasingly, associations are using education programming as a vehicle for maintaining autonomy and professionalism. Sponsoring continuing education activities helps associations retain oversight of program accountability and the standards of skill and knowledge that define good professional practice.

Business and industry are major providers of continuing professional education through their training and development function. Employer-sponsored educational activities for professionals working in an organization usually focus on work-related knowledge or skill training specific to that organization. Most frequently, these educational activities include job orientation, training in performance skills, and preparation for jobs with greater responsibilities.

Finally, private vendors, human resource development consultants, and a variety of other independent providers offer their own expertise to assist professionals. Often they satisfy a specific learning need that leads to more effective professional practice.

In an expanding market in which substantial revenue may be generated, influence is exerted, and institutional prestige is at stake, providers of continuing professional education need to evaluate and strengthen their positions relative to other providers. The first step in developing a competitive strategy in this market is to assess the competitive climate to determine whether independent programming or some form of collaboration will produce desired results.

Assessing the Competitive Climate

Cervero and Young (in press), in their discussion of interdependence, provide a useful analytical framework for assessing the competitive climate that exists among providers of continuing professional education. Providers are interdependent—that is, they take each other into account in the marketplace while pursuing their own institutional goals—in varying degrees. Cervero (1986) identifies six strategies along a continuum with high degrees of interdependence (collaborative relationships) at one end and low degrees (competitive relationships) at the other end.

The first and most competitive strategy is monopoly. This occurs when there is only one provider in a service area, or when the provider is the only one that can program in a certain content area. For example, a state may mandate continuing education for a particular occupation, such as police work or tax assessing, and contract with an institution of higher education to provide the required training on an exclusive basis.

Parallelism is a market strategy in which the providers are engaged in similar activities but each ignores what the others are doing. Interdependence is low or nonexistent. In some communities, there are several colleges and universities providing nontraditional degree programs at night or on weekends to counselors and other professionals. Each provider offers a program based on its own perceived strengths, irrespective of what other providers may be offering.

A third market strategy is direct competition. Competition exists when service providers are engaged in similar activities, they are aware of one another, and the goal of each is to maximize its share of the market. For example, in the intensely competitive field of noncredit management development workshops and seminars, independent consultants, employers' training departments, professional associations, college or university business departments, and continuing education units all offer management-related courses with the full knowledge that others are offering similar programs. Each provider programs independently of the others and seeks a larger share of this lucrative market.

A fourth strategy is cooperation, which involves service providers coming together in a joint relationship on an ad hoc project-by-project basis. Informal sharing of mailing lists or program speakers among providers is an example of this strategy.

Coordination is a fifth market strategy in which service providers agree to cooperate rather than to compete. In one example of coordination, an engineering professional association, the state department of transportation, and the engineering school of a university cosponsored a program on bridge construction for practitioners. In the coordination strategy, the providers take one another into account in a formal and consistent way, each contributing specified resources to achieve a common goal.

The final strategy is collaboration, in which providers enter into a highly interdependent, usually long-term relationship involving agreed distributions of power, status, and authority. Collaboration occurs when there is either a formal contract or an informal agreement between two or more continuing professional education providers to work together in serving a particular client group. For instance, a majority of accredited medical schools in the United States cosponsor ongoing continuing medical education programs with community hospitals.

According to Cervero (1986), the choice of a market strategy depends on the relationship that exists among various actors and the social and political dynamics that motivate them to engage one another. To understand the relationship, providers should ask: What incentives must exist before cooperation will occur between service providers? Does one provider have the expertise, resources, and relationships to dominate a particular market? Can two or more service providers complement one another's resources and join forces to dominate a market segment? Can an extra-organizational force influence a strategic outcome? For instance, might a state legislature contract with one institution to provide mandatory continuing professional education?

Competitive Planning

Wherever a provider falls on the interdependence continuum, the relationship with other providers is just one aspect to be considered in developing a competitive strategy. Achieving a competitive advantage over other continuing professional educators necessitates an internal decision to pursue a strategy of cost effectiveness, differentiation, or focus (Porter, 1980, pp. 9-33). This in turn requires that the provider distinguish itself from the competition by establishing plans and goals that capitalize on particular strengths. Perhaps most important, a provider of continuing professional education must recognize that it is part of a service industry, with all that this implies for attracting and retaining clients.

> Systems that deliver successfully consist of well-thought-out jobs for people with the capabilities and attitudes necessary for their successful performance; equipment, facilities, and layouts for effective customer and work flow; and carefully developed procedures aimed at a common set of clearly defined objectives. They provide sufficient capacity to meet most commonly experienced levels of demand efficiently. They can help reduce customers' perceptions of risk. And the delivery systems themselves often help insure that standards for service quality are met, that services perceived by customers are differentiated from the competition, and that barriers to competitive entry are built [Heskett, 1986, p. 20].

Competitive planning for continuing professional education can enhance the probability of achieving an effective service program and educational delivery system. The following discussion considers the basic elements in a competitive plan.

Commitment to Service Excellence. In the provision of educational programs, as in other service industries, expressed and operational values, commitment of staff who deal with the public, and managerial philosophy of the organization are of utmost importance. An educational program that is well received because of teaching excellence and attention to administrative details (such as convenience of location and physical comforts) makes an impression of high quality. Participants are inclined to remember the provider and enroll in further courses.

The "customer driven" organization, first popularized by Peters and Waterman (1982) and since studied by a host of researchers, has become almost a management cliché. The attenuation of this ideal is the first step toward the decline of any people-intensive business. The development of a successful competitive strategy in the education of professionals begins with the nurturing of a service culture within the providing organization.

A service culture is a function of an appropriate internal milieu, in which the organization's espoused values coincide with its operational behaviors and activities. In addition, a service culture depends on the effective delivery of educational programs whose supporting personnel embody the organization's commitment to quality and excellence. Finally, a service culture is exhibited by a managerial philosophy and practice that reinforces this internal environment and by strategic decisions that foster both client satisfaction and employee support.

Summarizing the importance of an internal commitment to service excellence, Heskett (1986, p. 134) cites direct relationships between:

- The design of successful service encounters—through employee selection, training, customer preconditioning, facility layout, efficient equipment, and other efforts—and service employee satisfaction
- Management emphasis on serving customers (instead of imposing rules and procedures) and service employee satisfaction
- Successful service encounters and service employee motivation
- Satisfied service employees and satisfied customers
- Satisfied customers and an increased volume of business.

A competitive advantage will accrue to those providers of continuing professional education that establish and implement effective human resource management practices in their pursuit of educational excellence.

Market Segmentation and Positioning. Providers that focus their efforts on the instructional programming that they do best are often in a position to achieve cost economies as well as high standards of educational quality. Identifying what they do best begins with market segmentation. In the process of market segmentation, the provider identifies both a specific market and a program, level of service, or system of instruction suitable for that market segment. Positioning is a related concept: The provider considers the relationship among its own characteristics, those of the targeted market segment, and those of the likely competitors. Taken together, these two concepts establish a basis for identifying particular groups of consumers with enough characteristics in common to make possible the design and development of an instructional program that meets client needs, is competitive, and is based upon what the provider can do best.

An example of effective segmentation and positioning is the case of a small college business department that wanted to enter into the noncredit continuing professional education market but lacked certain resources, such as institutional recognition and faculty expertise, critical to competing with more prestigious schools in the area. After deciding not to compete directly with the other schools' more lucrative executive development programs, this school actively pursued small and medium-sized businesses and industries that had training needs but limited resources. The college designed a program that targeted first-line supervisors and middle managers. It was successful, because the college identified a neglected market segment and positioned itself to capitalize on what it could do well for that segment.

Establishing a competitive position in continuing professional education requires research in market segmentation and positioning that addresses questions such as: What educational program does a specific clientele need or want enough to pay for? To what extent do competitors provide these programs? How can our organization best segment the market and then serve the various segments? To what extent are our capabilities differentiated from those of our competitors?

This phase of competitive planning requires a market research function. Such a function is common in many business enterprises, but it is not common for most continuing professional education providers. Instead, this function most often takes the form of a simple needs analysis or a survey assessing client educational interests. However, the most successful and best-managed continuing professional education programs in the future will be those that incorporate a market research function that systematically tests the institution's resources against client needs and interests. New program concepts will be refined and tested until there is strong evidence of a match between provider capabilities and market demand.

Focused Operating and Geographical Strategy. A focused operating strategy begins with a clear business definition, one stated in terms of anticipated results for clients. The business definition, often an organizational mission statement, should not be so narrow as to restrict entrepreneurial risk taking, but also not so broad that it permits activities beyond operational competence or ability to control.

An example of a rather brief, limited statement of purpose is as follows:

> The Department of Continuing Education is the central deliverer of continuing education to the adults of the state

and region. It seeks to extend the resources of the College through educational programs that are responsive to the needs and interests of adult learners.

Focus is a function of the institutional resources and internal capability of the education provider. The provider must have a well-defined body of knowledge and expertise in a particular field of practice (for example, medicine, law, or real estate) and, of utmost importance in providing continuing professional education, the ability to transmit this knowledge to an adult population. A focused statement of purpose can be developed by addressing questions such as: What is our overall goal? What are our future targets? What is the desired future state of our program? What are the qualitative or quantitative objectives that we will strive to meet? What mix of cost, program differentiation, and internal capabilities can lead us to maximize our results?

In his discussion of focus in service industries, Heskett (1986) observes:

> An examination of the business definitions and product portfolios of a number of the most successful service firms suggests that they seek to focus their efforts on customer segments, internal capability, geographic dominance, or some combination of these. While focus is not always reflected in their respective business definitions, it is implicit in what they do, the products they develop, and the businesses they acquire [p. 77].

The choice of a geographical strategy depends on the provider's delivery system network. Specific considerations include economies of scale associated with the geographical area served and the nature of competition within the provider's chosen delivery area. For an urban university to market a continuing professional education program locally is far different from its marketing that program in a larger geographical region. As the geographical area served expands, the mix of competitors increases significantly. Time and cost are important to learners in any locale, and the provider must be able to compete on these scales in every market it enters.

The decision to offer local, regional, or national continuing professional education programs depends on:

- *Product appeal.* Is the program needed and wanted, and will it attract a sufficient audience?
- *Institutional support.* Will the course be self-sustaining, and if not, to what extent is the organization willing to support it financially?
- *Risk-taking ability and entrepreneurial skill.* What is the probability for success and what are the consequences of failure?

- *Marketing skill.* Can the institution efficiently, effectively, and persuasively promote the program to the right people?

Carefully defining a particular geographical area in terms of client density and potential to participate can result in higher market share and an increased ability to respond rapidly to requests for additional instructional programs, and can thereby justify the institutional investment.

Establishing Partnerships and Coalitions. It is easy to underestimate the power of partnerships and coalitions in securing a more favorable competitive position. Yet intentionally seeking out organizations to assist in the design, delivery, and sponsorship of educational activities creates a networking effect for gaining a competitive advantage that one cannot afford to overlook.

Partnerships, or joint ventures with one other organization, can range from occasional ad hoc, informal arrangements to much more formal, institutionalized relationships in which policy and procedures govern and clearly define joint activities. The astute program manager may use partnership as a short-term business strategy to co-opt potential competitors and produce a built-in source of potential educational consumers. Coalitions are series of relationships established by a provider to assure a market segment for any given education activity. Coalition, as opposed to partnership, is a longer-term strategy whereby the provider seeks to carve out a secure market position by linking together several compatible organizations with a common goal and the willingness to share responsibility for and authority over programmatic decisions.

An example of a successful short-term partnership would be a university provider that joins with a professional association to deliver a single educational program for the association's members. Another would be a university that cosponsors a major conference with one or more other colleges or universities. The result of such ventures is reduced competition and a greater opportunity for success. In a long-term partnership, the provider systematically cultivates an enduring relationship. An example would be a university that actively and regularly solicits opportunities to provide educational support and assistance to a professional association. This sort of partnership is accomplished in a number of ways: by developing personal relationships, offering to conduct a thorough analysis of the educational needs of the association's members, providing assistance in workshop and conference planning, serving in an advisory capacity to the association's educational or professional development committee, and securing instructional resources not only from the university community itself but from any source the association's leadership deems desirable. In effect, the university provider intentionally promotes itself as the association's principal agent for systematically meeting the membership's educational needs.

A coalition exists when a provider facilitates a mutually acceptable arrangement among several organizations. An example would be a university's arranging with a state agency, a professional association, and an accrediting body to be the sole source of continuing professional education programs leading to relicensing or recertification. Such arrangements typically involve equal distribution of power, influence, prestige, and financial resources. However, the provider must be willing to sacrifice any of these, and some recognition, to retain its status as sole provider.

Program Quality and Price Value. The ultimate test for a successful competitive strategy in continuing professional education is in the consuming public's perceptions of the educational product as being of high quality for a good price. All participants in the educational activity have different demands and expectations, which makes it difficult for providers to predict behavior with any degree of regularity. Thus, in order to understand quality and price value in providing continuing professional education, it is necessary first to understand what consumers are looking for and how they evaluate their participation in educational programs.

> To state that service firms will have to develop service quality to be able to compete successfully is meaningless, unless one can 1) define how service quality is perceived by customers and 2) determine in what way service quality is influenced and which resources and activities have an impact on service quality, i.e., how service quality can be managed by the firm [Gronroos, 1983, p. 23].

In continuing professional education programming, a potential audience reads, hears, or views information on the course prior to making a commitment to participate. They may interact with members of the provider's organization, or they may be influenced by participants familiar with the provider's product (McCallum and Harrison, 1985, pp. 35-48). The potential consumer forms an image of the program provider and the educational activity by comparing his or her educational expectations with the perceived quality of the provider's program. The consumer's evaluation of the activity may or may not resemble any objective measure of its quality. When the consumer's image of the program or provider is distorted, it must be corrected. For example, there has been an increase in credit programs for professionals offered on weekends and at convenient locations such as shopping centers. A perception exists among some consumers and among other academic units that these programs are inferior. Providers of these programs must make a special effort to address questions of quality and academic equivalence both internally and with the consuming public.

What is quality in educational programming? Clearly, its definition varies with each participant, and it is influenced as much by expectations as by actual experiences. The ability to influence those expectations will vary inversely with the extent to which consumers have defined their expectations. Achieving quality continuing professional education programs results from intense efforts (1) to identify and to respond in a timely manner to consumers' perceptions of their training needs, (2) to influence positively the consumer's image of the providing organization and the programs it markets through promotional activities, (3) to structure the organization with a service orientation, and (4) to develop ample feedback opportunities and incorporate the feedback into one's operating strategy.

Cost management in continuing professional education involves pricing the educational product not only to recover costs and perhaps earn a return on investment but also to reflect the perceived value of the educational product in the eyes of program participants. A competitive operating strategy must therefore be designed so that the value of the program as perceived by the educational consumer—and thus the price that can be charged—is sufficiently greater than the actual cost of supplying the product to allow an adequate return on investment.

Strategic Options

An effective competitive strategy for the continuing professional educator will take into consideration all the elements of competitive planning discussed above. It will attend to both internal issues such as organization, pricing, and service orientation, and external issues, such as competitors, perceived value of the educational program, and societal trends and issues (Lovelock, 1984; Normann, 1984). Several specific strategies have already proved their effectiveness in the continuing professional education marketplace.

One strategy is to standardize educational programs to the greatest extent possible, while still ensuring that they do not appear to be "canned" or mass produced. Offering to various client groups standardized curriculum packages covering such subjects as motivation, communication skills, and customer relations allows for cost efficiency in the delivery of programs without the sacrifice of educational quality. These interchangeable curriculum modules must be tailored to specific groups through prior needs assessments and the integration of relevant examples and supporting materials.

Another strategy is to customize continuing professional education programs for specific market segments. For example, a patient care course would be relevant to many professions in the health field; a seminar that addresses the management of highly skilled technical workers can appeal to a variety of client groups in a highly technological market. This strategy enables the provider to develop a competitive advantage by matching its strengths with the learning needs of a diverse market segments.

Closely managing the supply of programs according to consumer demand is another competitive strategy. The essence of a supply/demand strategy is to offer only those high-quality educational programs that are cost effective and targeted to the learning needs of a specific group. Achieving this objective requires skillful program management—analyzing the potential market, carefully pricing programs, accurately predicting program expenses, and determining the number of participants needed to break even or produce a return on investment.

Another way to gain a competitive advantage is to seek every opportunity to involve the educational consumer in the planning, design, and delivery of continuing professional education programs. A client who feels like a part of the educational process—rather than an object of it—has a stake in its success. Actively involving the client group in programs gives one an advantage over competitors because of the relevance, credibility, and official sanction that comes with client group affiliation. For one provider, affiliating with the local secretarial association and involving some of its members in designing an educational program for secretaries had a positive impact on program relevance and credibility. Furthermore, if the association were to become a formal cosponsor, the provider would gain a market ally in offering an officially sanctioned program and thereby extend the reach and impact of its publicity efforts. In addition, incorporating members of the group in some instructional capacity enhances the program's responsiveness to participants (assuming that those selected possess the necessary instructional skills).

Another competitive strategy is to develop specialized certification programs for various occupational groups. A certification program is any structured curriculum designed around a specified content area with a mechanism built in for systematic evaluation. Certification is not intended to assure competent performance by professionals but instead attests to program participation and exposure to a defined curriculum. Components of a certification program should include:

- A regular client group with a stake in the provider's program over a specified period of time
- An educational program that is capable of addressing a specialized area of professional practice
- Participant recognition upon completion of a standardized curriculum.

A certification program is most effective when the provider is affiliated with a particular occupational group and is recognized by that group as the primary source of continuing education for members. For instance, thirteen states, some in cooperation with institutions of higher education, offer their supervisory and management personnel a series of intensive management seminars that, upon completion, results in the designation Certified Public Manager, considered by some to be the state management equivalent of the Certified Public Accountant designation (Henning, 1981, pp. 69-72).

A final strategic option is to use market data and technology in the provision of continuing professional education. For example, market research indicates that there are many potential participants, eager to take advantage of educational programs, who encounter such obstacles as inconvenient program location and the lack of perceived relevance to learning needs. Providers that utilize innovative technological delivery systems to reach these consumers will have a decisive marketplace advantage. Interactive videodiscs, adult learning laboratories, interactive teleconferencing, self-help videotapes, and even personal computers open up a world of information available through various subscription services and electronic bulletin boards. Programs that incorporate such new instructional technologies will be favorably positioned over the long run.

Summary

This chapter has addressed a key element in competitive strategy for providers of continuing professional education: a logically organized plan for analyzing existing strengths and resources in order to gain a competitive edge and to fortify a competitive position over the long term.

As more and more occupations professionalize practice, the need for continuing professional education will continue to increase. Likewise, the number of educational providers will increase, each of them vying for a particular service niche. Effectively competing in the field of continuing professional education is contingent upon the provider's mapping a strategy to plan, motivate, and manage all resources and activities having an impact on educational consumers. The cornerstone of a competitive strategy is the ability and willingness to organize institutional assets to deliver high-quality programs and make them available to a specific professional consumer segment. This requires a commitment to excellence by providers and a dedication to the concept of public service.

References

Cervero, R. M. "Interdependence in Continuing Professional Education: A Research Perspective." Paper presented at the American Association for Adult and Continuing Education Conference, Hollywood, Fla., October 22, 1986.

Cervero, R. M., and Young, W. H. "The Organization and Provision of Continuing Professional Education: A Critical Review and Synthesis." In J. C. Smart (ed.), *Higher Education: Handbook of Theory and Research*. Vol. 3. New York: Agathon Press, in press.

Gronroos, C. *Strategic Management and Marketing in the Service Sector.* Marketing Science Institute Report no. 83-104. Cambridge, Mass.: Marketing Science Institute, 1983.

Henning, K. K. "Certification as a Recognition of Professional Development." *State and Local Government Review*, 1981, *13* (2), 69-72.

Heskett, J. L. *Managing in the Service Economy.* Boston, Mass.: Harvard Business School Press, 1986.

Hohmann, L. "Professional Continuing Education: How Can the Professional Associations and Other Providers Best Interact?" In M. R. Stern (ed.), *Power and Conflict in Continuing Professional Education.* Belmont, Calif.: Wadsworth, 1983.

Houle, C. O. *Continuing Learning in the Professions.* San Francisco: Jossey-Bass, 1980.

Lovelock, C. H. *Services Marketing: Text, Cases, and Readings.* Englewood Cliffs, N.J.: Prentice-Hall, 1984.

McCallum, J. R., and Harrison, W. "Interdependence in the Service Encounter." In J. A. Czepiel, M. R. Soloman, and C. F. Surprenant (eds.), *The Service Encounter.* Lexington, Mass.: Heath, 1985.

Normann, R. *Service Management: Strategy and Leadership in Service Business.* Chichester, England: Wiley, 1984.

Peters, T. J., and Waterman, R. H., Jr. *In Search of Excellence.* New York: Harper & Row, 1982.

Phillips, L. E. "Is Mandatory Continuing Education Working?" *Mobius*, 1987, *7* (1), 57-64.

Porter, M. E. *Competitive Strategy.* New York: Free Press, 1980.

Stern, M. R. (ed.). *Power and Conflict in Continuing Professional Education.* Belmont, Calif.: Wadsworth, 1983.

John F. Azzaretto is assistant administrator, Governmental Training Division, at the University of Georgia's Carl Vinson Institute of Government/Georgia Center for Continuing Education. He also directs the Georgia Center Kellogg Project to establish a Council for the Improvement of Continuing Education for the Professions.

Most continuing higher education providers cannot compete in the direct mail, mass marketing arena; they need a strategy that takes advantage of their particular strengths.

Contracting with Business and Industry

Richard B. Fischer

Estimates of the amount of money spent by business and industry on training employees vary widely, depending on the source of information. Spending may be in the range of 30 billion to 80 billion dollars per year. Whatever the amount, the market potential is huge. While the majority of these funds support in-house training conducted by business and industry for their own employees, the remaining 30 to 40 percent purchased from outside vendors is a strong lure for universities and colleges. Of course, it is also a strong lure for a multitude of other providers. In every community, there is a plethora of continuing education providers serving business and industry. Fast-food chains run their own "hamburger colleges." Local professional associations offer seminars to members. YMCAs, city departments of parks and recreation, local school districts and the Small Business Administration offer courses in a wide variety of subjects. Real estate and insurance firms provide training to recruit new employees or entice the public to use their services. Private training consultants spring up like wildflowers. Large corporations employ full-time training directors or bring in training from their national headquarters. And major national seminar firms such as Fred Pryor, Career Track, and the American Management Association use sophisticated mass mailing techniques to reach local businesses and organizations.

Colleges and universities that want to get into training need to understand the complexity and competitiveness of this marketplace. Continuing higher education institutions must find strategies appropriate to their academic strengths and position within the community. This chapter will focus on strategies that have proven effective.

Advantages of Contract Training

As one authority (Elliot, 1986, p. 1) states, "With the entry of high-quality, low-priced national providers, the public seminar/conference market has become increasingly competitive." These providers for the most part operate on the basis of a direct mail, mass advertising strategy. They mail large numbers of fliers, 30,000 to 40,000 pieces minimum, into each city, expecting 1 to 2 percent registration return. Each flier incorporates multiple cities and dates so that printing runs are large, often in the millions, thus reducing the per-unit marketing and mail preparation costs. Sophisticated computer techniques are used to merge, purge, and sort a variety of mailing lists. Seminar topics are usually limited to those with wide appeal, such as "Improving Your Managerial Effectiveness." Entry into this marketplace is easy because of the absence of barriers, as discussed in Chapter Two.

Most continuing higher education providers cannot afford to compete in this direct mail, mass marketing arena. They do not have the computer support to take advantage of economies of scale. Most educational institutions are also not willing to invest the risk capital necessary for major mass marketing activities. Many feel such marketing activities are incompatible with their missions and perhaps even detrimental to their academic reputations.

An alternative strategy to the direct mail, mass marketing of open enrollment seminars is to concentrate on contract training with business and industry. In contract training, continuing education activities are designed to meet the unique needs of a specific business firm. Enrollment is restricted to employees of that business. Frequently the training is done at the business site. The educational institution, in partnership with the business, develops the content and secures the instructional resources. The business recruits the participants. In traditional open-enrollment continuing education programs, marketing and promotional costs to recruit students can often amount to 40 to 60 percent of the program budget. These funds are sunk or risk costs, since they are incurred even if the program is cancelled (Fischer, 1986, p. 76). Contract training, in contrast, minimizes the amount of marketing and promotional dollars that must be spent. It is a strategy of minimal risk to the educational institution.

Strategic Questions

The development of any competitive strategy revolves around three critical questions (Gup, 1986, p. 218), which continuing education providers that decide to focus on contract training must keep in mind.

1. *Where are you going?* As discussed in Chapter One, the institution that tries to be all things to all people ends up satisfying no one in the long run. Thus, it is important to envision a clear set of outcomes for any strategy. Is the goal to increase income, expand markets, increase enrollments, minimize risks, minimize development time, expand geographically, or enhance the image of the institution? Whatever the goals, they should be clearly articulated, understood by everyone in the institution, and supported by administrative policies and practices.

2. *What is the environment?* What are the internal financial and political constraints within which the continuing education unit operates? What is happening in the national economy? Is the local economy growing, stagnant, or declining? Are area businesses reducing in size? Are plants closing?

For the astute provider, plant closings present opportunities to provide contract seminars on career search or résumé writing. Helping terminated employees to assess their skills, identify new employment opportunities, or retrain not only has social value but provides an important service to industry and union organizations. Equipping valued employees with new skills allows them to retain their jobs as production processes change technologically. For example, several automobile manufacturers have initiated major training contracts with colleges to teach robotics and digital equipment repair to employees who otherwise would have been laid off.

3. *How do you get there?* What are the specific actions that should be taken to reach the goals?

Higher education institutions that succeed in competing for contract training have several characteristics in common. They have a systematic approach to initiating contact with business and industry. They sell contract training just as an industrial salesperson sells specialized chemical compounds. They spend most of their time outside the academic environment, in the client's office or plant. Repeated visits and ongoing communication are essential.

In addition, successful competitors for training contracts commit resources to the development of long-term relationships, often at the expense of short-term opportunities. This may mean weeks or months of visits without any contract income. Relationships are given time to develop; pushing for quick sales is avoided. Hours are spent with the client in surveying, planning, and designing model training programs.

The client is encouraged to send representatives at no charge to preview courses and interview faculty. Monies are spent on travel and on possible training aids.

Quality is enhanced at every opportunity, and great attention is given to small details. Faculty inexperienced in teaching adults are coached in new instructional approaches. Instructional technologists are hired to improve presentations. Audiovisual aids are prepared professionally instead of run off at the last minute on office copy machines. Handout materials are typeset, organized, and placed in notebooks.

Customer relations is given more than lip service. Telephone callers are greeted warmly and given accurate information. Telephone messages are returned promptly. Last-minute changes in clients' needs (adding two additional people, starting one hour later) are accommodated willingly. These little services make an important difference. One major mid-Atlantic university lost a major corporate client when, on short notice, the client requested an overhead projector and the university refused, not because the equipment was unavailable but because the required two weeks' notice had not been given.

How many colleges take the time to train their registration personnel, telephone operators, janitors, and security and food service personnel in good customer relations? Quality, timeliness of service, customer relations, and price/cost value are cornerstones of successful competitive strategies (Bevelacqua, 1985, p. 8).

Competing for the Client

"The marketplace of business, industry and professionals is different in many ways from the marketplace of individual students. It is a highly competitive marketplace with a well-developed business protocol" (Bevelacqua, 1985, p. 6). In order to compete successfully for contract training, educational institutions need to understand what the purchaser considers important in selecting a provider.

Timeliness. The ability to respond quickly to requests from clients, stay on schedule, and commit sufficient time to do a high-quality job is critical. The continuing higher education provider needs to approach business in a consulting mode and time frame, as opposed to a traditional academic mode and time frame. Many successful vendors adhere to some version of the "eight-hour rule": Within eight hours (one day) of an initial inquiry from business, the program planner should visit the business site and become aggressively involved in designing a program to meet expressed needs.

Results Orientation. Programs must be practical and problem centered. Although there is a definite place for the liberal arts in the business world, business and industry are most commonly concerned with improving the bottom line. Theory and philosophy must take a back seat to the building of skills. Simply stated, when businesses want to know how to tell time, they do not generally want to pay to learn how to make a watch. This does not mean that theory is not important. It does mean that more attention needs to be paid to understanding what is important to the client and to starting the relationship at that point.

Contractor Relationships. For the most part, businesses are not interested in one-time arrangements with vendors. They are interested in long-term relationships in which the parties can benefit from learning each other's strengths. Such relationships involve open, ongoing dialogue and joint participation in the design of training programs.

Value Versus Price. Two important points are worth noting about these decision criteria. First, price is *not* the most important criterion. Second, perceived value *is* the most important criterion. Businesses are most concerned about whether the institution can deliver what it promises and whether available resources are sufficient to do the job. Higher education institutions, thinking that price is the deciding criterion, often undervalue the planning and design skills that they bring to the program development process and underprice their contract training. This results in cutting corners to save money. But of course quality may be adversely affected by efforts to minimize cost. This is counterproductive in working with business and industry. The best strategy is to build the finest program possible and price the program to generate sufficient resources to support top quality.

Consulting Versus Marketing Skills. Too often continuing education providers are eager to respond to business needs with packaged answers. Programs should be custom designed. Off-the-shelf, packaged programs are not well received by business. Industry is seldom interested in sales pitches about the standard programs the educational institution has to offer. Rather, business and industry are interested in having the educational institution listen and learn about business problems and needs and then determine what educational resources may be available to help solve these problems.

It is also important to understand corporate budget timetables. Training scheduled to suit the availability of faculty during Christmas vacations may be ill-advised if the corporate budget year ends December 31. Instruction must be available in different formats and at odd times. One institution in the East has been successful in offering training at the end of the midnight shift.

The continuing education provider should also own or be able to arrange for equipment and facilities that training programs may require. Personal computer training is flourishing because educational institutions have the latest hardware and software in sufficient quantity to train large groups of employees. The *Directory of Conference Facilities and Services*

(National University Continuing Education Association, 1985), a compilation of meeting facilities and services available through colleges and universities, indicates the importance of training facilities as a competitive tool for recruiting corporate clients.

Barriers to Success

Once the provider understands the buyer's criteria for purchasing contract training, it becomes apparent that there are three major barriers to success.

Procedural. Continuing higher education providers tend to be reactive rather than active. Very few educational institutions have a systematic approach to contacting area businesses and industries to learn about their problems and needs. Marketing by personal contact should replace or enhance the hit-or-miss direct mail approach used by most educational institutions (Fischer, 1984, p. 3). Failing to be timely after the client has been approached is among the biggest obstacles to success. Continuing education providers must be more accessible, respond faster, and follow through in order to establish the long-term linkages desired by business.

Attitudinal. Too often higher education institutions end up competing with themselves. Faculty work through institutional channels and also free-lance outside the educational institution. Colleges and departments within the same institution unknowingly compete for the same business. Institutions sell their names to national seminar brokers who control the decisions of content and faculty selection, normally the prerogative of the educational institution. Clearly such lack of coordination and control is not in the long-range interest of the educational institution as it competes for contract training.

Academic. Most business problems are interdisciplinary in nature and do not fit neatly into the traditional academic department structure. Loyalties to academic disciplines and the lack of problem-centered curricula hinder the ability to compete for contract training.

Suggested Approach

Some of the barriers indicated above can be overcome by initiating a systematic approach to working with business and industry. The following model can serve as a guide to program developers as they call on business and industry.

Step 1: Initial Face-to-Face Contact. Initiated by the continuing education administrator, this first visit to a business is not to seek commitment but to listen to needs and explore ideas. This step does not usually involve faculty and is undertaken at no cost to the client.

Step 2: Second Contact. Once a problem is discussed or a need identified, a team-building and problem-solving session follows. This session should include potential faculty presenters, continuing education personnel, and a representative group of the business's employees who are involved with the problem. Ultimately this latter group will be the students in the contracted training program. This session should allow everyone to take responsibility for the problem and the proposed educational solution. At this meeting continuing education personnel should explain how they work, the role of the client, and costs and fees.

Step 3: Proposal Development. As a result of the problem-solving session, a customized proposal is developed that includes a statement of the perceived problem, the draft of the training schedule and curriculum, any additional problems the business may need to address but which the program will not cover, logistics, and financial arrangements.

Step 4: Presentation to Committee. Proposals should never just be mailed to the client. They should be presented to the same group convened in Step 2. The provider should go into the meeting with the assumption that the program is sold and present the proposal accordingly.

Step 5: Conducting Program or Pilot Program. A pilot program is one that is entirely new for the continuing education provider or is the first in a series of programs being developed for the client. Because of its experimental nature, it will probably be revised after the first offering and the provider should pay particular attention to evaluating the pilot program.

Step 6: Evaluation of Results. Present a three- to four-page written evaluation to the planning committee to discuss effectiveness. Plan for the repeat of the program or program sequel in a way that builds on competencies gained in the first training program.

Competing with the Client

Continuing education providers frequently find themselves in competition with the potential clients' own in-service training programs (Elliot, 1986, p. 25). Not only do these in-service programs compete for training dollars; in some cases they represent precisely what the corporate training director was hired to do. Proposals by an outside vendor to duplicate existing in-service training are obviously threatening. This explains why educational institutions often have more success selling training to plant supervisors and line management than to personnel managers or training directors.

Positive Approaches. There are several approaches to this problem. The first is to distinguish training needs that the client's in-house program is well equipped to serve from needs that the continuing education provider can serve more advantageously. A strong case can be made that educational institutions can more efficiently and effectively provide training in areas common to all organizations, such as supervisory training, team building, and interpersonal communications. The client's in-house program can better focus on areas specific to the given company, such as financial management or accounting procedures.

The second approach is to point out the ability of the educational institution to handle the detailed paper work of training programs. This service can free the time of the client's training director for higher-level activities.

The third is to cite the following advantages of engaging the services of the higher education institution:

- Up-to-date educational materials: Higher education institutions are usually among the first organizations to become aware of new publications and training materials.
- Access to a wide variety of resources and expertise: Higher education personnel interact regularly with faculty at other institutions and staff of various professional and trade associations, as well as a wide range of industrial personnel.
- Use of college training facilities: Many businesses have conference rooms, but few have special facilities designed to enhance the learning process.
- Ease of locating and contacting instructors.
- Access to a new employee pool: Developing relationships with colleges may lead to campus recruiting, placement of students, or referrals of talented graduates.
- Expenses paid through tuition benefit plans: Training can be treated as a fringe benefit without the need for special funding requests.
- Documentation of training through college transcripts: Employees benefit from having permanent records of both credit and noncredit instruction.
- Prestige of college-associated program: A university or college name usually means additional recognition.
- Availability of adult education expertise: Corporate training personnel may not be familiar with androgogical concepts or the current research on how adults learn.
- On-site advising, registration, and assessment of training needs.
- Client support of the local education community: The town-gown relationship, as well as the local economic base, can be strengthened by industry-university training partnerships.

Finally, joint sponsorship of programs may also be an enticement to training directors. They may value their association with the university and perceive it as tacit approval of their methods and in-service programs.

Minimizing Cost Objection. Sometimes, in defense of its own on-site programs, a business protests that buying contract training from outside vendors is too expensive. In many cases the claim is not accurate, because the client is comparing the total cost of the outside purchase with only the out-of-pocket costs of in-service programs. When personnel time and fringe benefits are included in the calculation, it may in fact be cheaper to use an outside vendor. Interestingly, as businesses have focused on cost containment, outside vendors have benefitted. Many businesses have eliminated internal training departments or started to charge intracompany fees for training. In the latter case, the intracompany fees are often higher per person than fees charged by outside educational institutions.

Competing with Yourself

To vary the famous quote from the comic character Pogo, We have met the competition and it is us. As mentioned earlier, one of the major barriers to success for educational institutions competing for training contracts is the lack of coordination within the institution. This includes both the failure of the institution to act as a unified entity and the competition between the institution and its faculty who may also be operating on a free-lance basis. This is the most serious problem the educational institution faces. If a strategy of pursuing contract training is to be successful, it must be supported by appropriate internal policies and procedures. Some of these are suggested below.

Internal Organization. The business client wants a single access point that can represent the resources of the entire educational institution. This necessitates some centralization of the continuing education function. There is no single model that is best. The entry point can be a college, a separate department, or a designated central administrator. The latter two offer the advantage of not being loyal to specific academic disciplines.

Faculty Compensation. Institutions must provide incentives to encourage faculty to work through the institution, not independently. Obviously, compensation is an issue. Most institutions have some restrictions on the amount or rate of compensation faculty can earn from continuing education activities. The rationale for these constraints is to "protect" the faculty so that they are not diverted from teaching and research activity. There are two fallacies in this rationale. First, good faculty can accomplish all these tasks and more; weak faculty cannot accomplish the work irrespective of any institutionally imposed financial constraints. Second, most of these constraints are handled by central administration and thereby diminish the ability of deans and department chairs to manage faculty workloads. While it makes sense to provide guidelines assuring consistency in the rate of pay, it is counterproductive to dictate broad overload compensation levels. This kind of policy forces good, energetic faculty to engage in independent activities outside the institution.

For faculty, the question about the rate of pay is not how much they are being paid but whether they perceive that they are receiving their fair share. If faculty are to join and remain loyal to the continuing education program, they need to share in its financial successes. More and more, institutions are paying faculty on a sliding scale rather than a flat per-day or per-seminar rate. Faculty may also be interested in rewards expressed through increased travel funds, new computer equipment, and so on.

Conflict-of-Interest Policy. Continuing educators also need to be aware of the existence of conflict-of-interest policies that affect outside employment. Most institutions have such policies but ignore them. Although faculty should be encouraged to engage in consulting, group instruction is not consulting. This is the primary business of the educational institution. The distinction between consulting and teaching needs to be clarified. Some institutions have also instituted noncompetition clauses in faculty contracts to assure exclusive access to faculty resources in a prescribed academic or geographical area. Such arrangements may be legally questionable, however, and are at best hard to monitor.

Internal Communication. Successful contract training also relies heavily on effective internal communication. Each segment of the institution, including central administration, should be kept current on industry-related training. The development office may be able to coordinate its efforts with successful continuing education activities. Alumni affairs personnel may provide valuable leads on alumni in decision-making positions in industry. The placement office always welcomes more recruiters. These relationships make contract training desirable in the eyes of others in the institution. In some cases (for example, leads from the alumni office) they offer a potential competitive advantage for the college-based provider.

Using Competitive Advantages

Higher education organizations have a number of competitive advantages over other providers of training. Two key advantages are stability and price/cost effectiveness.

Business and industry want to be assured of a dependable source of training just as they want dependable suppliers of other goods and services. While consultants and other vendors come and go, higher education institutions remain a constant presence. They are not likely to go bankrupt. They are not likely to relocate in the sunbelt. This stability allows for a continuity of training resources. Because most institutions have multiple faculty in any discipline, there is instructional back-up in case of illness, retirement, or relocation of any individual trainer.

The educational institution also has an advantage because of its multidisciplinary base. As mentioned above, few business problems fit neatly into the province of a single discipline. For example, it takes the combined efforts of business, psychology, and communications to deal with small-group behavior. The educational institution also has a competitive advantage because its incentives for educating people go beyond financial return: A college is often willing to respond to needs that for-profit providers will not address. Some incentives in addition to financial incentives for the college to become involved in contract training are:

- Increased institutional visibility: Employees of business firms who otherwise may not have cared about the higher education institution become students and friends of the institution.
- Enhanced reputation: Training of high quality reflects favorably on the institution as a whole and can improve not only further contract training opportunities but also undergraduate and graduate admissions.
- Benefits for faculty: Contract training often leads to consulting or research opportunities for faculty; it also provides the faculty an opportunity to bring real-world problems and situations back into their regular classroom teaching.
- Creation of new faculty positions and opportunities: Funding from contract training can be used to supplement salary budgets or, when training is part of the regular load, to subsidize faculty positions.
- Increased community service: Contract training for agencies such as United Way is not necessarily financially lucrative but does provide service opportunities for the college.
- Identification of new academic markets: Contract training can develop into new curricular areas, which in turn often lead to new academic degrees; for example, the law enforcement training of the 1960s resulted in many new criminal justice degree programs.
- Involvement in economic development efforts: In Delaware, for example, the availability of training was a key element in the Financial Redevelopment Act that successfully attracted financial services industry to the state.
- Increased political support: Institutions seeking increased state funds can point to their training activities with local industry as an illustration of their contribution to the state's economy.

At different times, any or all of these may serve as effective arguments in convincing internal constituencies of the benefits of involvement in contract training. These incentives also give the college a competitive advantage because they allow the college to focus on long-term commitments to performance instead of short-term financial survival.

Of course, the college is also interested in financial returns. Contract income can be used to generate surplus funds, to recover some general overhead, to fund faculty positions, or to offset operating losses. However, income is seldom as critical to the college as it is to a private provider. Whether the college is state supported (with a subsidy of administrative salaries and expenses) or self-supporting, it usually operates from a lower cost-position than the commercial vendors. Similarly, the general lack of the need for a return on investment means that the college can opt to compete on the basis of price.

The provision of *high-quality* continuing education programs should, of course, be the only prerequisite for success. Attention to detail is the corollary to this prerequisite. Business protocol should dictate procedures, and timeliness is often a more important criterion than cost from the buyer's perspective. Knowledge of these considerations may be the most important competitive advantage in obtaining contract training.

References

Bevelacqua, J. *Working with Business.* Manhattan, Kans.: Learning Resources Network (LERN), 1985.
Elliot, R. D. *Marketing In-House Seminars.* Manhattan, Kans.: Learning Resources Network (LERN), 1986.
Fischer, R. B. *Personal Contact in Marketing.* Manhattan, Kans.: Learning Resources Network (LERN), 1984.
Fischer, R. B. "Pricing and Fee Management." In H. Beder (ed.), *Marketing Continuing Education.* New Directions for Continuing Education, no. 31. San Francisco: Jossey-Bass, 1986.
Gup, B. E. "Begin Strategic Planning by Asking Three Questions." In J. W. Pfeffer (ed.), *Strategic Planning.* San Diego, Calif.: University Associates, 1986.
National University Continuing Education Association. *Directory of Conference Facilities and Services.* Washington, D.C.: National University Continuing Education Association, 1985.

Richard B. Fischer is associate director for statewide program development and marketing with the Division of Continuing Education at the University of Delaware.

Using telecommunications to move from a local to a state or national marketplace in continuing education requires cautious risk-taking.

Telecommunications as an Element of Competitive Strategy

Barbara Gellman-Buzin

Continuing education students often shop for learning; they want the best products, easily accessible, flexible in hours, and generally responsive to the demands of the busy adult. If they cannot fill their educational needs through one provider, motivated learners will search for another. Learners who have demands that are not met locally may very well turn to a provider offering services from a distance—through the mail or electronic media.

Telecommunications is the most obvious manifestation of the move away from the traditional student sitting at the foot of the scholar. In a competitive environment, scholars are reaching out to students, meeting them on their own territories if not in their own homes. Geographical boundaries that once protected providers from competition by outsiders no longer do so. Students, in turn, are increasingly coming to expect learning resources far from home to be made available to them.

Providers can react to the telecommunications movement by withdrawing and becoming intimidated or by becoming strategic leaders through technology. Faced with cost considerations and a complex array of technical possibilities, providers are asking, What is in it for me? This chapter will address that question by suggesting a process that will help the provider determine how best to use those resources we place under the umbrella term *telecommunications.*

Telecommunications Literacy: What Business Are We In?

Providers are often confused about the terminology encompassed by telecommunications, and confusion leads to misinformation or total avoidance. For purposes of this discussion, *telecommunications* is defined as the systems available for the delivery of information between points. The information may be in the form of text, audio, or video communications, or a combination of these. The various formats of telecommunications range from the simple audiocassette to increasingly complex long-distance networks. In selecting any form of telecommunications for learners, providers must ask, What content messages do I want to deliver? and *then* determine the best method of delivery.

The complexity of telecommunications is notorious. The name of the popular video game company, Atari, translates from the Japanese as "prepare to be engulfed!" (Singleton, 1983, p. 1). Just as the first-time video game player is somewhat awed by the mechanics of the system, so are providers of continuing education overwhelmed by the systems available to them. Rather than becoming intimidated and losing the competitive advantage, providers can meet telecommunications as a challenge and an opportunity. Perhaps more than any other programmatic or structural decision, that concerning telecommunications should be approached gradually, knowledgeably, and with a healthy curiosity that insists, This innovation will not control our institution; it will assist us in reaching some of our goals more quickly and efficiently.

Video. As the exploration of telecommunications begins, the provider should keep in mind the three major areas of service—voice, data, and video communications. Video systems include satellite teleconferencing, videotapes, videodiscs, national broadcast networks, teletext, and combinations of these. All video systems may deliver information delayed or live. Many are one-way communications systems, and others, such as videodiscs, are interactive.

Voice and Data. Voice telecommunications include telephone networking, audioteleconferencing, and closed-circuit audio to complement video presentations. Voice systems may be intricate, long-distance telephone networks or simple, local campus systems. Data transfer telecommunications includes electronic mail, telefacsimile, and computer networking. Data may be linked to telephone, microwave, fiber, or satellite equipment through a computer with a modem and dedicated line. The limits to developing a voice-and-data system are (a) costs and (b) imagination.

Applications. Applications for each telecommunications format are numerous. The following is a partial list of suggestions for applying the technology to continuing education: professional seminar teleconferences, association meetings by teleconference, satellite or microwave transmission of outstanding experts/professors from distant locations, prepackaged courses for individual use in libraries, interactive videodiscs that allow printing a picture of the program, two-way interactive communication with instructors in different cities, telephone connections to libraries for reference purposes, course offerings accessible to home computers through local telephone numbers, and electronic bulletin boards posting offerings from providers at distant sites.

The above examples demonstrate that providers may opt for telecommunications systems for both instruction and marketing. If some providers have turned to telecommunications, it is because they have noticed "signals" in the environment suggesting that (a) learners' needs are changing and (b) the economics of the marketplace are changing. Consider the examples in the following section.

Environmental "Signals" for Telecommunications

Expanding Knowledge Base. The knowledge base is expanding in a way that makes it virtually impossible for learners to keep abreast of their professional fields. Lawyers are a good example of professionals who just do not have the time to settle into a library for the hours needed to research changes in the law. Yet the consequences are grave for the client whose attorney is not aware of recent legal rulings. Telecommunications can become a major source of support for this profession once providers develop a data base that is accessible in the lawyer's office and that will, in effect, do the research for him or her. Library work no longer has to be time consuming. Unfortunately, systems such as this still are not readily available when and where the users need them.

Need for Access. Professionals in rural areas are another major audience for telecommunications continuing education. Country doctors have the same continuing medical education requirements as their urban counterparts, but they do not have access to programs. Providers using telecommunications to reach these areas will undoubtedly become those professionals' key source of ongoing continuing education. Lack of access is a critical problem for many professionals; a solution may be a variety of telecommunications services.

Deregulation. The breakup of AT&T opened the doors for the building of local area and long-distance networks, both providing telephone and data services. A continuing education provider that serves a number of cities may choose to invest in its own telephone system, thereby saving the costs of long-distance communications. Such networks expedite voice-

and-data exchange among the administrators, instructors, and the students in the service area. A local area network lends itself to creating an infrastructure of which the student is a vital part. Imagine the student unable to leave his or her place of work enrolling via this system through a designated computer at the company. Ease of enrollment alone may give the provider the competitive advantage.

Demanding Workplace. The workplace is demanding more on-site training of employees. This increased demand may lead a provider to consider developing a video network capable of sending courses to a company, hospital, military base, or other fixed location that employees cannot leave. Just as extension and outreach programs have traditionally brought instructors to those sites, telecommunications can do so without involving travel time or taxing limited training personnel pools.

Recognizing that these signals in the environment are important, long-term changes, some providers have turned to telecommunications. They have discovered ways in which telecommunications bridges distances, extends possibilities for interaction between learners and support personnel such as guidance counselors and librarians, and brings the benefits of increased markets and high-quality instruction.

National Applications

National University Teleconference Network. Continuing education providers using telecommunications on a nationwide scale include the National University Teleconference Network (NUTN), headquartered in Stillwater, Oklahoma. NUTN brings together a variety of higher education institutions, businesses, and nonprofit organizations through satellites located across the country. To receive NUTN's programming users require downlink satellites, which can be purchased for a few thousand dollars or much less, depending on services needed. Those organizations serving as program transmitters require uplink satellites, which are more expensive but are a good investment if the number of learners served is sufficient.

Programming available through NUTN is created by providers ranging from the Campbell Soup Company to veterinary schools, state government agencies, the American Management Association, and hotel corporations. One Holiday Inn teleconference reached over 16,000 employees in 134 sites (Oklahoma State University Educational Telecommunications Services, 1984). This programming allows corporations to train hundreds of employees nationwide for a fraction of the cost of on-site seminars. Savings in travel costs are a major benefit of teleconferencing.

Providers using NUTN as a delivery system exemplify the competitive advantages of satellite delivery. Professional associations reach larger numbers of members than before and thereby increase the impact of the association's services. The result is likely to be more satisfied members, who will seek training from the association rather than from other providers that are unable to offer coordinated programs of continuing professional education, journals, and conferences. Associations use telecommunications to help create the image of a "one-stop" provider—a network serving as the sole source for continuing professional education.

Colleges and universities reach beyond their traditional classrooms, expanding enrollment without proportionately increasing staff. An instructor may train veterinarians from all over the country with nearly the same amount of preparation time required for a typical on-campus course. There is money to be made by the strategically positioned provider of noncredit activities mandated by the professions. Colleges and universities providing programming can improve their overall quality by reinvesting those dollars in their traditional programs.

Corporate providers are, in effect, taking care of their own employees, bypassing other providers. Where companies once depended on local colleges, they can now find suitable commercial training programs that can be delivered by satellite. Resources formerly allotted for tuition to outside providers can be reallocated.

National Technological University. Another leading national delivery system is the National Technological University (NTU), consisting of twenty-two member engineering institutions. NTU is a private, nonprofit organization founded in 1985 to serve the advanced education needs of engineers, scientists, and technical managers. NTU is governed by a board of trustees, predominantly scientists and technical engineers. Universities providing programs to NTU include Stanford University, Polytechnic Institute of New York, and the Massachusetts Institute of Technology. Participation in such a prestigious organization can build the image of a provider and thereby attract more traditional and nontraditional students. Outstanding programs can transcend the participating provider's geographical limitations, increase enrollment, and bring in funding for the provider's on- and off-campus programs.

NTU's parent organization is the Association for Media-Based Continuing Education for Engineers (AMCEE), which demonstrates the effectiveness of a strong professional association in telecommunications. AMCEE is a consortium of engineering colleges, formed in 1976. NTU offers more than 4,000 hours of academic credit instruction; AMCEE provides over 1,500 hours of noncredit, state-of-the-art programming. Commercial businesses, along with governmental agencies and the AMCEE membership, provided initial funding. Other professional organizations considering telecommunications can use this AMCEE/NTU model in developing strategic plans.

Telecourses. Paralleling national telecommunications systems are those videocourses prepackaged for use by local providers. A typical videocourse contains twenty-six to thirty half-hour lessons, a study guide for the student, a textbook, and a faculty manual for managing the course. Telecourses, as these programs have become known, developed as a result of local providers' seeking ways to meet needs—for example, a community need for basic core curriculum courses (English, history, or art) unmet because of limited resources. Telecourses deliver the educational content, while the local provider serves as contact.

Colleges using telecourses appoint campus instructors, but these faculty only grade papers and meet a few times with the students. This arrangement allows increased enrollment with limited costs. Telecourse videotapes can be viewed through the Public Broadcasting Service (Adult Learning Service), cable channels, and state or local microwave networks, or they can be viewed independently in libraries. The local continuing education provider or college leases the right to offer the course materials and during a given semester may show each program unlimited times. The most cost-effective delivery system is through the Public Broadcasting Service and specifically through a consortium purchase. A consortium of colleges or other continuing education providers may be regional or local, depending on the nature of competition within a certain geographical area. The cost of leasing or purchasing a telecourse decreases greatly with other consortium members sharing the expenses.

Dominating telecourse use are two-year institutions, according to a study by the Corporation for Public Broadcasting (Riccobono, 1986). This may be due to the fact that major telecourse producers are organizations such as the Dallas Community College District, Miami–Dade Community College, and Coastline Telecourses, and most programs are lower-division level. Providers interested in reaching a nationwide audience are determining which courses are most needed to expand the telecourse base. Not only can production be profitable (if a number of users lease or buy the courses) but it can also enhance the image of the producer's home institution. The Dallas Community College District, for example, is known nationwide through the marketing of its telecourses. In the past few years, telecourse producers have asked other institutions to participate in funding the productions and then have shared the profits of the course.

Telecourses are high-quality programs, a far cry from the tedious days of "Sunrise Semester." But the use of programs produced outside a home institution has important policy implications. Providers must remain cautious in their offerings so as not to diminish the credibility of the home institutions. A well-produced telecourse should have a strong curricular foundation, reflecting the contributions of a team of experts. As a result of concern for telecommunications quality, the Council on Postsecondary Accreditation and the State Higher Education Executive Officers (Project ALLTEL, 1983) have proposed a set of guidelines for offering such courses. The guidelines suggest ways to regulate local offerings, national programs, and interstate commerce of telecommunications for learning. These guidelines will offer some protection for local providers in establishing distant learning programs.

State and Regional Applications

Oklahoma: Statewide Microwave. Many states and regions use satellite delivery, telecourses, microwave systems, and other media mixes to offer continuing education programs. Oklahoma, for example, in 1971, began operating a statewide microwave system developed in response to business, educational, and individual needs.

With statewide access to higher education as the Oklahoma system's primary goal, quality production became a secondary consideration, so that its telecourses are not comparable to the more polished, packaged telecourses available from other providers. Its willingness to accept lower quality production results in important cost savings. The Oklahoma system provides both color and black-and-white transmission to over sixty sites in the state from ten transmitting institutions. A simple production studio with two still cameras offers one-way video and two-way audio, and has been dubbed "talkback television." Similar systems exist on a smaller scale in other locations, including Texas.

The emphasis in Oklahoma is not on glittery television production but rather on extending the campus. The advantage to this extension is that unmet needs can now be served. Providing institutions increase enrollments at low cost; distant learners develop associations with particular providers and subsequently may take more courses on campus. Administrators at these providing institutions may, therefore, increase the resources for those divisions offering courses in order to maintain high-quality instructors and support services.

In 1985, the Oklahoma State Regents for Higher Education decided to build on fifteen years of success by expanding the network—originally video with an audio component—to include voice-and-data services. Funding will provide increased video potential with a linkage to statewide public broadcasting, satellite, and production facilities. Through a cooperative arrangement with the state government, much of the Oklahoma system may use fiber optics. The conversion of this simple microwave system to a more complex network with a variety of delivery options makes the project very exciting. Over 2,000 voice-and-data channels will provide a statewide telephone network, computer linkage, library data base exchange, telefacsimile, and electronic mail. Providers will serve higher education, businesses, correctional institutions, military bases, and public libraries. Providers are encouraged to assess needs, propose offerings to the state regents, and participate in scheduling. Providers use the system to extend proven campus courses rather than to offer first-time courses. The regents' staff serve to coordinate efforts among providers, monitoring competition to assure that each provider gets the most for its programs without encroaching on others. It is the provider who grants the credit, receives the tuition, and increases enrollment.

In Oklahoma, a major evaluation of the use of the system is under way. Traditional on-campus courses may be pushed aside for other offerings—courses by professional associations and other noncredit programs. It is the large-scale audience, located in many sites, that needs the system most. Courses for part-time students and continuing professional education are very likely to take over a major portion of the schedule. Higher education institutions do not pay to use the network; professional associations do. The costs of maintenance may very well lead the state regents to balance the offerings between those who pay and those who do not. Telecommunications systems are often driven by economic decisions, which is something all providers should consider when first considering technology.

Texas: Regional Microwave. On the regional level, the TAGER-TV system in the Dallas-Ft. Worth area provides courses to higher education institutions and industry. Four Instructional Television Fixed Service (ITFS) channels, microwave links, and cable television provide graduate-level engineering courses, computer science courses, business courses, and other offerings to the region. Texas has established certain rules which raise interesting policy questions for providers. A "one-third" rule limits off-campus offerings that can be taken to complete a degree program. So, in effect, many providers' hands are tied with respect to credit offerings through telecommunications. This situation suggests that professional associations, businesses, and other non-academic providers will eventually gain a competitive edge over higher education providers if policies continue to limit the use of telecommunications for academic purposes. Non-credit activities using technology do not raise the brows of doubting administrators the way credit courses using technology do.

Wisconsin: Audio. University of Wisconsin Extension provides professional education courses via a dedicated four-wire audioconferencing network with slow-scan, freeze-frame television. Still pictures of the instructor are offered along with slides and graphs (Zigerell, 1984, pp. 19–32). Providers can use audioconferencing for training or meetings at a very reasonable cost to each site. Strategically, incorporating such a system gives a company another method of training, eliminating the need to go elsewhere for the service. Providers of continuing professional education can, for example, use this technology to bring experts from all over the country into a single program.

Pennsylvania: Cable with Microwave. The Pennsylvania State University has a regional cable network with microwave connections. The system is currently being upgraded. It will eventually provide an extensive media mix and involve the collaboration of a variety of providers from business and education. The Pennsylvania State model serves as a good example of ongoing strategic planning and risk taking through new technologies.

Providers interested in cable transmission can gain a competitive advantage by developing rapport with the local cable company manager and, most important, getting everything in writing at franchise renewal time. Cable operators have not been obligated to offer air time to providers since deregulation, but they are interested in increased subscriptions. Providers should point out to the cable operator the advantages of specific continuing education programs. For example, if continuing legal education programs were offered on a designated cable channel, lawyers could be contacted through direct mail to subscribe. The lawyers would have the service, providers would collect income from training materials that accompany the video programs, and cable operators would have a monthly income from the subscribers.

California: Instructional Television Fixed Service. The Stanford Instructional Television Network (SITN) is administered through Stanford University's School of Engineering. It provides graduate education to several thousand professional engineers, managers, and other employees at 140 San Francisco Bay area companies and research institutions. It is interactive, with one-way video (provided through microwave ITFS), and a two-way audio system.

SITN stands out as a leader in using telecommunications for continuing professional education. Providers can approach businesses with a proposal for a training program and solicit start-up monies. The high-quality programming of Stanford's traditional courses gives them a strategic advantage based on image. Businesses want that prestige, but they do not have the time to send employees to the campus. The arrangement is reasonable in cost, since corporations help with funding.

New Mexico: Fiber Optics. One system that began with state-of-the-art technology is New Mexico Tech Net. It covers the Rio Grande Research Corridor with a 300-mile public and private sector communications network utilizing a fiber optics system. The network links research scientists, engineers, two national laboratories, a national polar observatory, the Air Force Weapons Laboratory, White Sands Missile Range, numerous high-technology corporations, and three universities.

The major objective of the system, economic development, is accomplished through a sophisticated computer network. Operated as a separate entity, New Mexico Tech Net brings together government, local business, and higher education. Unique to the system is a governance structure separate from each provider, with the operational goal of avoiding competition for control.

The above examples represent only a fraction of the telecommunications systems offering continuing education in the United States. In each case the local providers have decided to use telecommunications in the expectation that the quality and access demands, formerly unmet, will now be satisfied. Whether the provider capitalizes on specialization, access to prestigious programming, convenience to users, or flexible scheduling, all these variables combine to strengthen the provider's marketplace advantages. With these examples in mind, the provider can begin to ask, What's in it for me? and How do I go about planning for telecommunications?

Strategic Planning for Telecommunications

In considering telecommunications, a provider of continuing education should not become dazzled by the technology before considering several critical questions. Those providers that succeed are cautious risk-takers, an appropriate contradiction in terms for telecommunications leaders.

Providers should ask, What is the nature of the curriculum we wish to teach, and what do we know about the population of learners? Is individualized learning appropriate? What type of feedback do learners require? What is the course trying to accomplish? Is it visually oriented? Does it require delayed or immediate feedback? Does the instruction require self-paced or group-paced delivery? Are learners able to travel or must they stay where they are?

There may well be instances in which telecommunications is not appropriate and in which continued investments in traditional learning formats will provide the greater competitive advantage. If there are needs that could be well served through telecommunications, a decision to move in this direction is fraught with consequences for the provider's organization. Complex new issues of cost, staffing, collaboration, and competition arise. But if these issues can be dealt with, the provider may gain an otherwise unobtainable competitive advantage.

Administration and Faculty. Telecommunications will not succeed in any organization without top-level administrative support. Those colleges that lead in the technological marketplace have presidents who are convinced that telecommunications is good for the institution *and* for the president. At national conferences, it is often the president who boasts about the telecommunications programs offered through his or her institution. Such programs work with their support; they cannot work otherwise.

Faculty and trainers may resist telecommunications. These attitudes may be gradually changed with technical literacy training that demonstrates what is available to help in the teaching. Using telecommunications may mean more work for faculty and trainers, so it is critical to develop reward systems and incentives for their added efforts.

Before providers become embedded in strategic planning, it is advisable for them to participate in professional meetings with telecommunications experts. Leading continuing education associations have technology divisions that bring experts and newcomers together in the learning process. Visits to other providers who successfully use various forms of telecommunications are also helpful, as is actual participation in telecourses, teleconferences, or other activities that position the *provider* as the *learner*. As the provider participates, he or she can ask, What about this experience is enjoyable? What is difficult for me? What would the learners we are currently serving think about this? How could this environment for learning be improved? Would I want to take more courses this way?

Costs. Depending on the forms of telecommunications desired, the costs involved will differ. For tapes or telecourses, providers must consider the cost of leasing or purchasing as opposed to producing tapes, the cost of extra sets of tapes for individualized learning, faculty compensation, installation and operation of telephone lines for feedback, staff time (coordinators, counselors, admissions personnel), marketing, supplies for daily office work, mail, equipment for playing or airing tapes on television, travel, and consortium membership fees.

Some of these costs are visible to learners, and seem worthwhile in order to enhance learners' experiences with new delivery systems. Other costs are invisible to learners, but it is important that they not be ignored, because they are crucial to maintaining a high-quality program. Taken together, all these initial costs may far exceed what a provider originally anticipated. The advice of an experienced consultant is helpful in clarifying all the costs to be considered and in helping to weigh them against the advantages to be gained.

Other forms of telecommunications involve additional costs. Satellite delivery costs include purchases of a dish, transponder lease time, and other expenses such as the cost of repair and maintenance. Providers must purchase the more expensive uplink dishes; for users or local sites, however, receivers range from low-cost, non-steerable dishes to higher cost dishes that capture more signals. Providers of satellite programming must add in the costs of production and, if necessary, the building and maintenance of production facilities. Partnerships in satellite production prove particularly cost effective. Microwave dissemination and fiber optics include still other costs.

All costs for telecommunications should be developed in two stages: (a) administrative and (b) engineering and technical. Calculations of the return on investment should figure in savings potential (long-distance telephone rates may be eliminated, for example). It is advisable to retain a consultant to make equipment recommendations and cost estimates for individual systems and to oversee implementation.

Consortia. Smaller providers should either use lower cost systems or join other providers in consortia. Providers in a consortium can realize competitive gains. Members may also learn what to avoid and what to pursue in developing a communications program. Consortia work best when members complement one another by compensating for one another's weaknesses and combining their strengths. Joining the National Technological University, for example, gives local providers the opportunity to create networks with engineering training experts from across the country. Affiliation with the National University Teleconferencing Network gives the local provider exposure to excellence in production and marketing. Providers not only gain access to telecommunications leaders; they often emerge as leaders themselves.

Consortia help the local provider to become national through the exchange of programs among members, national distribution systems, and shared marketing costs. A local provider, formerly limited to offering a few core courses in a given discipline, may join other providers in delivering a full degree program. Consortia are effective in building systems, leasing or producing software, planning and development, and—perhaps most important—providing moral support in accepting risks and change.

Conclusion

Continuing education providers are coming to accept telecommunications as an inevitable part of the strategic planning process. Providers can succeed with economically sound systems, developed through long-term planning, needs assessment, market analysis, and evaluation. Leading providers of telecommunications match learning styles and instructional needs with delivery systems rather than selecting a technology based on its current popularity.

Providers can gain a competitive edge with strong telecommunications programs that have emerged from administrative support, grass roots support, effective media mixes, collaboration, coordination, attention to quality assurance, sound policy formation, and state-of-the-art networking where financially feasible. The assurance of continued support must be built in during the initial planning stages.

Providers will fail if their programs are based on weak curricular planning, random course offerings, ineffective organizational structure, lack of continued financial support, lack of administrative support, or the absence of continuous improvements and technical upgrades to guarantee quality.

Providers must be willing to risk in order to succeed, to fail in order to attempt change, to forgo traditional structures, and to accept challenges from everyone in decision-making positions. The local provider of continuing education is no longer protected by geographical boundaries or the travel limitations of the learner. To meet the challenge of serving the continuing education student of tomorrow, providers must rethink the entire format of their offerings. Telecommunications may very well be the answer.

References

Oklahoma State University Educational Telecommunications Services. "What Is Teleconferencing?" (videotape) Stillwater: Oklahoma State University Educational Telecommunications Services, 1984.

Project ALLTEL. "Joint Statement of the Accreditation, Authorization, and Legal Task Forces on Assessing Long-Distance Learning Via Telecommunications." Washington, D.C.: Project ALLTEL (Assessing Long-Distance Learning Via Telecommunications), 1983.

Riccobono, J. A. *Instructional Technology in Higher Education: A National Study of the Educational Uses of Telecommunications Technology in American Colleges and Universities.* Washington, D.C.: Corporation for Public Broadcasting, 1986.

Singleton, L. A. *Telecommunications in the Information Age: A Nontechnical Primer on the New Technologies.* Cambridge, Mass.: Ballinger, 1983.

Zigerell, J. *Distance Education: An Information Age Approach to Adult Education.* Information Series No. 283. Columbus, Ohio: ERIC Clearinghouse on Adult, Career, and Vocational Education, 1984.

Barbara Gellman-Buzin is acting vice chancellor for educational outreach for the Oklahoma State Regents for Higher Education. She has twelve years of experience in telecommunications, including applications in higher education, cable, and public broadcasting.

Collaboration can be useful in achieving several strategic objectives.

Collaboration as a Competitive Strategy

Hal Beder

This chapter discusses collaboration as a strategy for gaining a competitive advantage in the continuing education marketplace. This notion may seem strange to some readers, as much of the literature portrays collaboration as a cooperative strategy rather than as a competitive one. Within this tradition we are told that competition is harmful in that it breeds conflict, promotes duplication of services, and saps effort. Hence, cooperation rather than competition is the desired state. Collaboration, in this way of thinking, is a productive strategy for creating a cooperative environment.

While it is true that there are benefits to be derived from cooperation, it is also true that there are benefits to be gained from competition. Competition promotes educational quality and efficiency, as only those agencies that efficiently produce demand-satisfying programs survive in the marketplace. In an era in which continuing education has increasingly been expected to pay its own way and even to turn a profit, there is no doubt that a market economy has prevailed. In this atmosphere, one must compete to survive. Hence to pretend that competition does not exist is simply naive. Accordingly, this chapter will focus upon collaboration as a competitive strategy, not because it is philosophically more pleasing to do so but because it is simply more realistic to do so.

Forms of Collaboration

There are several forms of collaboration that may serve as the building blocks of a competitive strategy: cosponsorship, referral, coordination/control, and donor relationships. In cosponsorship, the continuing education provider conducts joint programs with another agency, the two generally sharing both costs and benefits. For example, it is quite common in continuing professional education for continuing education agencies to cosponsor conferences and courses with professional associations.

In a referral relationship, an agency refers clients to the continuing education provider. For instance, a local day care center might refer prospective day care providers to colleges that offer programs leading to required certification.

In a coordination/control relationship, the continuing education provider joins with other organizations to manage the organizational environment in mutually advantageous ways. As Beder and Darkenwald (1979) note, county-wide coordinating councils in New Jersey often provided a forum for "carving up the turf." In this case, the county vocational school informally agreed to offer vocational courses designed for the blue-collar trades, and the county college agreed to focus on white-collar vocational courses. In this way, pernicious competition was avoided, and each provider was left free to exploit a market without interference.

In a donor relationship, an organization provides an outright gift to the continuing education program, generally in expectation of obtaining intangible rewards such as publicity and the public's goodwill.

Strategies

This chapter focuses on collaboration as a strategic tool rather than looking at collaboration as a good in its own right. Any strategy must begin with a goal in mind and a plan for obtaining it. Collaboration is useful in attaining at least five objectives: domain extension, co-optation, cost reduction, risk reduction, and powerful alliances.

Domain Extension. As Benson (1975) notes, the domain of a continuing education provider is the sphere of influence in which it is legitimately permitted to operate; this is similar to what is popularly referred to as "turf." For example, the domain of a medical school's continuing professional education program is non-degree medical education. Domain generally derives from organizational mission but may also be legally mandated. Domain is generally defined by the content of programs one is permitted to conduct, but it may be delineated by other factors as well, such as geographical setting or types of clients served.

A continuing education provider's domain is one of the most important ingredients in defining which markets it will serve, for the provider invites trouble if it seeks to serve markets outside its domain.

Such trouble may come in many forms. Exceeding domain generally puts continuing education providers at odds with their parent institutions, which perceive the domain violation to be in conflict with organizational mission. Consider the consequences if a continuing medical education program were to decide to offer recreational courses in physical fitness. In conflicts with parent institutions, continuing education seldom wins. Thus, obvious domain violations should be avoided.

Trouble may also come from outright war with competitors. Although competition is the norm, it should not be hostile. Generally speaking, the competition in continuing education proceeds according to an informal set of rules commonly understood by providers. One of these rules is that it is acceptable to compete within one's domain but unacceptable to transgress another's domain. Consequently, domain transgression often invites competition of an abnormally hostile and bitter type. Since in such cases the transgressing continuing education provider necessarily operates in a new, unknown market, hostile competition greatly increases risk. Thus it is usually unwise to move into another provider's domain unless one has the wherewithal to compete with an established provider over the long term.

Finally, most domains are circumscribed by rules of a legal or quasi-legal nature. Sometimes the rules derive from the legal system itself, so that improper domain extension can lead to legal action. For example, in most states, by legal mandate the domain of granting bachelor's degrees resides solely with colleges and universities. Often, however, the domain constraints are imposed internally by the rules and regulations of the parent organization, for example, a prohibition on collaboration with for-profit firms, or a limit on the geographical area that a provider may serve. When such regulations are violated, the administrative reprisals can be dire.

Domain then provides the boundaries that define a continuing education provider's market. Occasionally, however, there are needs to operate outside one's domain. For example, because of domain restrictions, continuing education agencies are sometimes expected to operate in very lean markets. Community college programs in low income urban communities, adult literacy programs in affluent communities, and programs of all types in areas of low population density are examples. In such cases, breaking even may be problematic unless some source of profitable programming can be exploited outside the traditional domain. Similarly, a continuing education provider may possess a resource that is not prized within its domain but is highly valued elsewhere. For example, a university conference center established to serve the continuing education needs of the university might need to expand domain beyond the university community to remain profitable.

Cosponsorship, discussed above as a type of collaboration, can be an excellent and legitimate method of expanding domain in such cases.

The continuing education provider may simply cosponsor a program or programs with organizations within the restricted domain, flying the cosponsor's flag, so to speak. For example, an adult literacy program having difficulty because it is restricted to operating within an affluent community might cosponsor programs with the Cooperative Extension Service or other agency that operates on a county basis, and thus extend its domain. The university conference center that cannot fill its space from within the university community might induce academic departments to cosponsor residential programs with external professional associations.

Use of collaboration to extend domain into areas from which a provider is normally restricted can be a very helpful strategy if used sparingly. Obviously, however, if this strategy is carried to an extreme, the mission of the continuing education provider becomes compromised.

Co-Optation. Through co-optation, the continuing education provider defuses competition by loosely assimilating competitive programs into the continuing education unit. Beder and Smith (1977) cite a good example. In a city in upstate New York, the director of a comprehensive adult learning center had just acquired a new facility with a surplus of space and was seeking to further penetrate the adult literacy market. At the same time, a local church in the vicinity had decided to mount its own literacy program in direct competition. Rather than engage in outright competition, however, the director made his excess space available to the church program, which conducted classes under its own name for about a year. After that time, however, the church realized that operating its own program served no purpose. It disbanded, giving strong support to the program which had co-opted it.

Another example demonstrates the point. At an eastern university, the continuing education division of a graduate school of education found it difficult to function in a very lean market. To remain profitable, promotion costs had to be reduced. In the same school there also operated a grant-funded vocational education resource center, which was mandated to provide continuing education to the personnel of elementary and secondary vocational schools. The markets overlapped to some degree, as the graduate school's continuing education division was empowered to serve vocational education as part of its mandate.

To preclude competition in the vocational education market and to increase its public visibility by associating the graduate school's logo with its own, the vocational education resource center offered to disseminate the continuing education program's brochures along with its regular first-class mailings to all school administrators in the state. Although aware that it was being co-opted, the continuing education program was pleased to make the deal, since it benefited by saving thousands of dollars.

In employing co-optation, it is important that the co-opting agency plan for the co-opted party to benefit from the strategy, and it is generally wise to be forthright about one's intentions. Otherwise, the co-opted organization is likely to feel exploited, and once this happens, the co-optation is apt to be short lived, with rancor ensuing.

Cost Reduction. Perhaps the most beneficial use of collaboration as a competitive strategy is in the realm of cost reduction. Clearly, for a provider to remain competitive, costs may not exceed income, and, of course, the lower the costs, the lower one may set prices and thereby increase one's competitive advantage even further. Nearly all the forms of collaboration previously discussed can reduce operating costs.

Cosponsorship is a case in point. In cosponsorship, the continuing education provider typically supplies instruction and facilities while the cosponsor provides the learners. This obviates the need for promotion, which is usually the most substantial sunk cost incurred in programming. In using cosponsorship as a cost reduction strategy, it is important that the continuing education agency provide those resources that it has in greatest abundance—that is, which cost the least—while acquiring resources that it most needs and would otherwise have to pay for.

Valuable resources that continuing education providers typically have in abundance and can afford to contribute to a cosponsorship at little cost include planning expertise, skill in logistics, and a proven and respected reputation. Resources that are generally needed and should be sought from cosponsors include clients, presenters, promotion, and sometimes subsidizing funds.

Referral is another form of collaboration very useful in cost reduction. In a referral relationship, other organizations and satisfied clients refer clients to the continuing education provider, thus substantially reducing the provider's promotional expenses. In fact, the percentage of clients a continuing education provider receives through referral is one gauge of the health of the agency, for substantial referral generally indicates that programs are highly visible and well received by markets served.

Referral relationships should be consciously sought. In building referral relationships with organizations, one should look to agencies that complement the continuing education provider in mission. For example, one literacy program acquired most of its clients through referral from a state employment service. The employment service was rated on its ability to place its clients in jobs. Yet, many of those who sought assistance were too poorly educated to qualify for the jobs that existed. Furthermore, the employment service was prohibited by law from conducting educational programs. Thus it was quite willing to refer its poorly educated clients to the literacy program. Concomitantly, most of the literacy program's clients were investing in education to acquire jobs. Hence, once they had completed the program and were referred back to the employment service, the literacy program could claim that it provided job placement as well as education.

Donor relationships are an excellent way to cut costs, although this strategy is often overlooked. In continuing pharmacy education, for example, drug companies are only too happy to provide free speakers. Computer companies are often willing to provide free software and even hardware for continuing education activities. Corporations are frequently willing to provide free meeting space, and many organizations will provide free paraphernalia, such as T-shirts or registration packets, if these items carry their brand names.

Donations are rarely given for purely altruistic reasons, however, and the key to securing them is to clarify how the donation will benefit the donor. Pharmaceutical companies will donate free speakers and other assistance to continuing pharmacy and medical education because they hope to influence what doctors and pharmacists prescribe. Computer companies have been aggressive donors because, once a client learns on a particular machine, purchase is likely. Identify the advantage to the donor, and donation becomes a very viable cost reduction strategy.

Properly directed, coordination/control relationships can also reduce costs. In a coordination/control relationship, providers of continuing education collaborate to solve problems of common concern. Such actions typically promote efficiency and thereby reduce costs. In a previously cited example, Beder and Darkenwald (1979) chronicle this type of situation.

In New Jersey, in order to facilitate cooperation and reduce duplication of services, the state mandated that in each county the community college, the area vocational school, and other interested providers of continuing education form county coordinating councils. Since all providers were operating in a market economy, one role the council played was to create a forum in which providers could "carve up the turf," thereby guaranteeing that each would have access to a particular market without competition from the others. Reducing competition through agreement saved promotion costs and allowed each provider to set prices without fear of being undersold by other providers.

Risk Reduction. One of the most difficult problems associated with operating in a market economy is the necessity of incurring risk. For many public sector continuing education programs, risk is especially problematic because the rewards for taking large risks do not offset the losses. Most parent institutions expect continuing education at least to break even, and they become a little suspicious (or even worse, greedy) when there are substantial profits. Thus the normal reward for taking great risk—great profit—does not obtain to the same degree that it does in the private market. On the other side, large losses generally will not be tolerated by parent institutions even if the risk that produced them seemed justifiable.

Collaboration is a useful strategy for reducing risk. Cosponsorship, for example, typically spreads the risk between two or more parties. When vital resources, such as clients, are guaranteed in advance of program operation, risk is further reduced. Similarly, cosponsorship typically reduces sunk costs, such as advertising expenses. This is an important benefit, since incurring large sunk costs in the absence of guaranteed registration is one of the riskiest propositions of all. Finally, it has often been acknowledged that risk is greatest when one is operating in a new market with a new product (Willard and Warren, 1986). This risk can be reduced if the cosponsor has substantial experience with and credibility in the new market to be served.

Productive referral relationships help reduce risk, because in fee-financed programs every successful referral represents income. Registrations that come without the expense of large promotional campaigns clearly reduce risk, and a continuous flow of clients through referral enhances program stability.

Donor relationships obviously reduce risk since donated funds committed in advance of program development are a guaranteed hedge against loss.

Powerful Alliances. The final strategy in which collaboration can be used to advantage is that of building alliances. Much has been made of the marginality of continuing education (Clark, 1968; Moses, 1971). To a great extent, marginality derives from the fact that continuing education is almost always a secondary function for parent institutions. Hence, continuing education is generally tangential rather than central to the primary enterprise. One result of marginality is that continuing education typically operates in a poor power position and is relatively vulnerable unless measures are taken to reduce vulnerability. Collaboration can help through the building of powerful alliances with cosponsors and other collaborating agencies.

The experience of a suburban public school continuing education provider is a case in point. This particular provider had grown substantially under the support of an enthusiastic superintendent of schools. Yet the director realized that he was quite vulnerable; should the superintendent retire, he would lose his base of power. To preclude this possibility, the director began a systematic effort to build interagency alliances. Each year the continuing education program sponsored a catered breakfast for all cosponsors. Teachers and counselors were urged to learn the names of their counterparts in cooperating agencies and to contact them regularly on a first-name basis. "Never bad-mouth a collaborating agency" was a strict rule, and most important, whenever a collaborating agency was threatened, the director was sure to lend his support. As a result, the continuing education provider was able to build a base of power independent of its parent institution, and when the superintendent did retire, threats to the program were fended off with relative ease.

To be competitive, continuing education programs need organizational stability and a degree of operating autonomy (Beder, 1979). Power to thwart threats to the program is, therefore, critical. Forming alliances with collaborating agencies is particularly useful in this regard, as collaborating agencies, being external to the continuing education program, can often work behind the scenes in times of crisis.

Principles of Collaboration

At this juncture, we have discussed several ways in which collaboration can assist in gaining a competitive advantage. This leads to a central issue: How does one go about establishing collaboration?

Reciprocity. The most important principle of establishing collaborative relationships is that of reciprocity. In collaboration, each party gains something and each party loses something. For example, the time spent on negotiating collaborative plans is always lost, and both parties typically lose some autonomy as well. According to the principle of reciprocity, for a collaboration to be successful, all parties must gain more than they lose. Continuing education should give what it values least, generally that which it has in abundance, while acquiring what it most needs. The same must be true for the other party. When all benefit more than they lose, the relationship will be stable; if this condition is not met, the relationship will be short lived.

Collaboration should be targeted. That is to say, careful consideration should be given to the needs of the continuing education unit, and collaborative relations should be sought specifically to meet them. In targeting, it is useful to consider which resources are most needed and which current resources are most expendable.

There are some resources that all continuing education agencies need: clients, facilities, instructors, expertise, power, visibility, and, of course, money. To a certain extent, which ones are most needed depends on the agency's stage of development. Newer programs are more likely to need clients and visibility, which are more difficult to obtain until the programs have been run successfully for some time. More established programs may need these resources as well but may choose to focus collaboration on gaining access to influence or funds.

As mentioned earlier, resources that continuing education providers typically have in abundance include prestige and expertise in planning and logistics. This sets the stage for a typical collaboration based on reciprocity. The dean of continuing education for a large community college wished to begin programming in a new market—real estate. Although competition for this market from private providers was intense, the market was expanding rapidly because of rapid population growth in the area. Upon reflection, the dean realized that the resources she most needed to enter the market were a guaranteed source of clients and credibility as a provider. Without these the potential for market development was poor.

Through a colleague, the dean learned that the local real estate association was having membership problems. Real estate brokers were reluctant to pay dues because they felt they were getting little service from the association. Obviously, the association was in need of activities to justify its existence. Although as one alternative it could mount its own continuing education program, it lacked the credibility and expertise to compete with private providers.

Potential for a reciprocal relationship existed. The community college possessed an abundance of programming expertise and credibility—just what the real estate association needed—and the association had access to clients and credibility in real estate. Realizing this, the dean contacted the association, and a productive cosponsorship was easily established.

Goal Complementarity. In planning for collaboration, it is generally most productive to focus on organizations that have goals and missions complementary to those of the continuing education provider rather than on those that have similar goals. Reciprocal relationships are likely to flourish in such circumstances. The above-cited example of adult literacy and the state employment service is relevant here. The employment service needed educated clients if it was to place them, but it was prohibited from offering its own educational programs. Likewise, the adult literacy program needed job placement but was not allowed to spend public funds to acquire it. Because the goals of the two agencies complemented each other so well, a two-way referral relationship easily resulted.

Costs of Collaboration. Although collaboration has many benefits, it also entails costs. The three most common costs are time, loss of autonomy, and organizational disruption.

It takes a considerable amount of administrative time to negotiate collaboration and then to maintain the relationship once it is established. This is most true for new programs that have not achieved visibility, for they must seek the collaborators rather than the collaborators seeking them. Time spent on collaboration can be significantly reduced, however, if collaborations are carefully sought with those agencies affording the greatest potential for success.

Autonomy, the second cost, is lost in nearly all collaborations, as the continuing education provider must relinquish some of its decision-making authority in the interest of the joint endeavor. This can become a severe problem when continuing education relies too heavily on one or two collaborations for a competitive edge. Collaborations should be diversified so that the program can afford to lose any one of them without dire consequences. In any collaboration, the scope of each partner's decision-making authority should be clarified in advance to avoid conflict.

Organizational disruption can occur when the activities of the collaborator interfere with those of the continuing education provider. In attempting to collaborate with public agencies managing programs under the Comprehensive Employment and Training Act, many community college programs felt that the constant priority shifts and bureaucratic red tape were not worth the disruption of their programs.

In avoiding costs, one of the critical considerations is the extent to which the collaborating organizations are linked. Linkage can range from informal verbal agreements to near merger. Although more formal collaborations may be more stable over time, they are also more difficult to terminate and are at least potentially more disruptive to the organization.

Summary

Collaboration in the form of cosponsorship, referral, coordination/control, and donor relationships can significantly enhance a continuing education provider's competitive position. These forms of collaboration are useful tools in five competitive strategies: domain extension, co-optation, cost reduction, risk reduction, and the building of interagency alliances.

In establishing collaborative relationships, it is important that each party gain more than it loses. Otherwise the relationship will be unstable and short lived. The best prospects for collaboration are organizations that have goals complementary to those of the continuing education provider, since there is a greater likelihood of a reciprocal relationship's thriving in such cases.

Although collaboration can provide many benefits, it is important to realize that costs are generally incurred as well. These costs include administrative time spent, some loss of autonomy, and, occasionally, organizational disruption.

References

Beder, H. "The Relationship of Community and Sponsor System Support to Selected Aspects of Adult Education Agency Functioning." *Adult Education*, 1979, *29* (2), 96-107.

Beder, H., and Darkenwald, G. *Occupational Education for Adults: An Analysis of Institutional Roles and Relationships*. New Brunswick, N.J.: Center for Adult Development, 1979.

Beder, H., and Smith, F. *Developing an Adult Education Program Through Community Linkages*. Washington, D.C.: Adult Education Association of the U.S.A., 1977.

Benson, J. "The Inter-Organizational Network as a Political Economy." *Administrative Science Quarterly*, 1975, *20* (2), 229-249.

Clark, B. *Adult Education in Transition: A Study of Institutional Insecurity*. Berkeley: University of California Press, 1968.

Moses, S. *The Learning Force: A More Comprehensive Framework for Educational Policy*. Syracuse, N.Y.: Syracuse Publications in Continuing Education, 1971.

Willard, J., and Warren, L. A. "Developing Program Offerings." In H. Beder (ed.), *Marketing Continuing Education.* New Directions for Continuing Education, no. 31. San Francisco: Jossey-Bass, 1986.

Hal Beder is associate professor of adult and continuing education at Rutgers University. For several years he directed the continuing education program of the Rutgers Graduate School of Education.

What must continuing educators keep in mind in order to create a sustainable competitive advantage?

Competitive Strategy: Themes and Issues

Clifford Baden

"As my back yard gets bigger, so does everyone else's back yard." So spoke a director of a continuing medical education program recently, reflecting on the changes brought about by technology. These changes made it possible for his programs to reach almost every physician in the United States. These same new opportunities, of course, were also available to most of his competitors.

Adult learners have many options from which to choose. Over the next few years, these options will increase. Additional providers will enter the field. Innovative collaborations among providers will result in the creation of entirely new programs. Technology will spawn many new learning options. Learning-plus-travel and learning-plus-employment programs will extend the reach of adult education to new audiences in new places.

The size of the market itself is likely to increase. Social pressures and financial incentives will urge providers to reach out to previously unserved clienteles. This is beginning to happen with certain ethnic groups, with illiterate Americans, and with blue-collar workers, especially the technologically displaced. These groups are still hard to reach, but they will be reached. The important questions for providers are: When, by whom, and how? Once they are reached, will they return for additional learning programs? Which providers will be most ready to serve them?

Competition is going to increase. Adult learners look at the number of offerings in the marketplace and perceive their situation as one of increased choice. Providers look at the same situation and see increased rivalry. If providers are going to attract and retain learners in this kind of marketplace, they must think clearly about what competitive strategies they will pursue.

This sourcebook has described three generic approaches to strategy. Cost leadership, differentiation, and focus are fundamentally different ways for a provider to think about how it is positioned in the marketplace and what it has to offer to learners. As one reads through the chapters on conglomerate providers, continuing professional education, contracting with business and industry, and the special opportunities afforded by telecommunications and collaborative ventures, several themes emerge. They can be articulated as suggestions to providers.

Challenge Conventional Wisdom

Many educators have recently come to recognize the dimensions of America's illiteracy problem. Which providers should be developing literacy programs? Certainly not all. The most discussed topic in continuing education in the late 1980s is how to sell programs to business and industry. Should every provider pursue this purportedly lucrative market? Of course not. Many will jump on these current bandwagons, and many will fall or be pushed off because they have not competed from a position of strength. When all other providers are chasing after the same golden fleece, it is time to step back and ask why we should be, too. Do we really have any sustainable competitive advantage? If not, forgoing short-term expediency in favor of a longer-term vision will pay off in terms of better, more consistent use of resources and a sustained, coherent public image.

As Pappas points out in Chapter Three, conventional wisdom holds that a provider should not use billboards as an advertising vehicle. For most providers, this may be good advice. But for the conglomerate provider following a differentiation strategy, it is poor advice. Indeed, the fact that billboards are effective for the University of Utah shows how successful that university's differentiation strategy has been. First, there are enough learners in the community who recognize the institution's name to make the billboard a cost-effective medium. Second, the university has differentiated itself so well that its name alone evokes positive responses from those who see the name on a billboard. Finally, even though a dozen different viewers might have as many different associations with the university, all those associations are positive and all are elicited by a simple message that reminds them that it is time to register for the new semester. It is true that for the many continuing education providers that follow a specialization strategy, billboards are inappropriate, as are full-page newspaper advertisements. But in the right community setting, they can be very effective as part of a differentiation strategy.

As another example, a few innovators are challenging the conventional wisdom that continuing education providers are limited to serving a small local market. Providers are discovering new ways to reach new learners around the country. Technology opens new doors for some providers; collaboration creates opportunities for others. Still others are carefully and advantageously combining multi-site local delivery with a single, centralized administration. All these providers are innovators and risk takers. If they succeed over the long term, it will be not because they were the "first ones out the door" but because they took risks within the context of a coherent, well-defined strategy.

Consider Collaboration

In his chapter, Beder outlines the various ways providers can use collaboration as part of a competitive strategy. Indeed, the theme of collaboration occurs repeatedly throughout this sourcebook on competitive strategy. Azzaretto writes about partnerships and collaborations in continuing professional education and the networking advantages they can bring. Virtually every example in Gellman-Buzin's chapter on telecommunications involves the collaboration of dozens of providers. The example of Elderhostel, cited in Chapter Two, involves collaboration among hundreds of college campuses.

Why collaborate? Collaboration can bring lowered costs and access to new audiences. It can also offer the advantage of prestige-by-association. From a competitive point of view, collaboration confers a powerful advantage when it involves an exclusive franchise—that is, when the provider is the only one in its area authorized to represent or work with its collaborators. The fundamental impetus for collaboration comes from the fragmentation of the continuing education field. A single provider finds it difficult, for structural reasons, to be in many different places simultaneously serving many different learners. A carefully crafted collaboration offers opportunities to increase outreach and expand market share.

Integrate All Aspects of Strategy

A strategy is much more than a mission statement. It reveals itself not only in the policy pronouncements of managers but also in operating decisions about which learners to serve, in which markets, at what locations, at what prices, and with what courses. It reveals itself as well in the behaviors that the organization rewards internally and in the quality of interactions with external groups. Strategy must be consistent. It must "succeed in knitting together the dimensions of intuitive dream, cognitive planning, organizational action, and market or historical outcomes" (Torbert, 1987, p. 96). When a strategic vision is shared throughout an organization, activity at each level will support and reinforce activity at every other level.

There are two common reasons why strategies fail. The first is "structural contradiction" (Bonoma, 1985). This occurs when the actions taken at one level of the organization are inconsistent with activities elsewhere in the organization. Sometimes this happens inadvertently. Too often it occurs because contradictory messages are transmitted at different levels, with the result that multiple strategies are implemented simultaneously at different places in the organization. The net effect is the same as no strategy at all.

The second cause of failure is overreaching. The flexibility that characterizes most providers of continuing education is a wonderful advantage; occasionally, however, it becomes a license to try anything at all. Some providers seem unwilling to choose a single strategy, discrete areas of competence, or a strong image to portray. They make a virtue of risk taking and experimentation when in fact they are simply avoiding hard choices. Resources are diffused. Different programs are launched for different audiences; many of these programs may be adequate, but none is outstanding. The end result is disappointing. Mediocrity in programming is quickly matched by mediocrity in market response.

What Kissinger (1979) writes about foreign policy is just as true for competitive strategy in any organization: "There is no escaping the need for an integrating conceptual framework . . . which 'links' events. . . . The absence of linkage produces exactly the opposite of freedom of action; policymakers are forced to respond to parochial interests, buffeted by pressures without a fixed compass" (pp. 114, 130).

Emphasize Quality

In another context, Beder (1987) has decried the effects of capitalism and empiricism on adult education: "The humanistic concept of the adult learner prevalent in the works of Knowles . . . and others is being replaced with the objectified notion of the adult learner as consumer. According to this way of thinking, the goal of program development is to establish the conditions whereby the consumer, a collection of traits and preferences rather than a person, is willing to exchange valued resources for the adult educator's 'product' " (p. 112).

Questions of competitive strategy in continuing education are in large part market-driven, it is true. Are we replacing the notion of the adult learner as a person with the notion of the adult learner as consumer? I think not. The dichotomy suggests an either-or choice, but it is possible simultaneously to acknowledge the relevance of both perspectives. Indeed, those providers who are most successful in their approaches to the learner as consumer are successful precisely because they respect the integrity and the needs of the adult learner as a person.

The authors in this book, all of whom are practitioners, make this point explicitly. Azzaretto writes about quality as a function of responsiveness to learner's needs, and he emphasizes an "internal orientation to service excellence." Pappas identifies the goals of "providing superior service" and "emphasizing a quality strategy." Fischer concludes that "the provision of high-quality continuing education program should, of course, be the only prerequisite for success." All of the authors in this sourcebook would argue that long-term strategic advantage accrues only to those who can consistently give adult learners what they need. Success in retaining adults as consumers comes to those who respect adults as individual learners.

Attending to learners' needs implies a constant alertness. Individuals grow and change; technology brings with it new patterns of behavior and new expectations; social customs evolve and values change. Every change offers new opportunities for the provider of continuing education. And with each new opportunity, the provider is tested: Is this really our area of expertise? What resources can we offer to learners? Is this consistent with what we have done before? If we start down this new road, will we be able to sustain a competitive advantage? Competitive strategy raises fundamental questions about competence and mission. These questions represent the stimulation and the challenge that await top management in continuing education.

References

Beder, H. "Dominant Paradigms, Adult Education, and Social Justice." *Adult Education Quarterly,* 1987, *37* (2), 105–113.
Bonoma, T. V. *The Marketing Edge.* New York: Macmillan, 1985.
Kissinger, H. *White House Years.* Boston: Little, Brown, 1979.
Torbert, W. R. *Managing the Corporate Dream: Restructuring for Long-Term Success.* Homewood, Ill.: Dow Jones-Irwin, 1987.

Clifford Baden is director of Programs in Professional Education at the Harvard Graduate School of Education and director of Harvard's Institute for the Management of Lifelong Education.

Index

A

Abell, D., 6, 17
Administration: for conglomerates, 33; and telecommunications, 80
Air Force Weapons Laboratory, and fiber optics network, 79
Alliance Française, specialization by, 14
Alliances, and collaboration, 91-92
American Association of Community and Junior Colleges, and economies of scale, 27
American Business Conference, 37-38
American Institute for Banking, specialization by, 14
American Management Association: and contract training, 59; and telecommunications, 74
Andrews, K. R., 6, 17
Ansoff, H. I., 31, 33, 34, 37, 40, 42
Association for Media-Based Continuing Education for Engineers (AMCEE), 75
AT&T, 73
Atari, 72
Azzaretto, J. F., 1-2, 45, 58, 99, 101

B

Baden, C., 2, 3, 5, 18, 19, 29, 97, 101
Bain, J. S., 33, 42
Baldwin Park Adult School, geographical flexibility of, 9
Bandwagon effects, of conglomerates, 34
Beder, H., 2, 85, 86, 88, 90, 92, 94, 95, 99, 100, 101
Benson, J., 86, 94
Berg, N., 31, 32, 33, 35, 40, 42
Bevelacqua, J., 62, 70
Bloom, P. N., 32, 33, 37, 42
Bonoma, T. V., 100, 101
Bower, J. L., 6, 17
Business and industry, contract training for, 59-70
Buzzell, R. D., 32, 33, 36, 37, 42, 43

C

California, Instructional Television Fixed Service in, 79
California at Los Angeles, University of, as conglomerate, 32
Campbell Soup Company, and telecommunications, 74
Career Track, and contract training, 59
Certification, and continuing professional education, 56-57
Cervero, R. M., 47, 49, 57
Christensen, C. R., 6, 17
Clark, B., 91, 94
Coalitions, for continuing professional education, 53-54
Coastline Community College, telecourses from, 76
Collaboration: analysis of, 85-95; forms of, 86; principles of, 92-94; reasons for, 99; strategies for, 96-92; summary on, 94
College Board, Office of Adult Learning Services of, 26
Competitive strategy: analysis of, 5-18; assessing climate for, 47-49; background on, 5-7; collaboration as, 85-95; concept of, 11; in continuing professional education, 45-58; for contract training, 59-70; and conventional wisdom, 98-99; in fragmented field, 19-29; generic, 11-16; integrated, 99-100; and market planning, 31-43; options in, 55-57; problems in, 16-17; questions in, 61-62; suggested, 98-101; and telecommunications, 71-83; themes and issues in, 97-101; variables in, 7-11
Comprehensive Employment and Training Act, 94
Conglomerates: advantages of, 32-37; analysis of, 31-43; competitive strategy for, 37-42; concept of, 32; summary on, 42
Consortia, for telecommunications, 81-82

Consulting skills, for contract training, 63-64
Continuing education: collaboration in, 85-95; competitive strategy in, 5-18; conglomerate, 31-43; and contract training, 59-70; as fragmented field, 19-29; future of, 97-98; professional, 45-58; suggestions for, 98-101; telecommunications in, 71-83
Continuing professional education: analysis of, 45-58; background on, 45-46; collaboration for, 86, 90; competitive climate of, 47-49; competitive planning for, 49-55; delivery context for, 46-47; strategic options for, 55-57; summary on, 57; telecommunications for, 73, 75, 78, 79
Contract training: advantages of, 60; analysis of, 59-70; approach to, 64-65; background on, 59-60; barriers to, 64; competition for, 62-64; competitive advantages in 68-70; and in-service programs, 65-67; and institutional competition, 67-68; relationships in, 63; strategic questions for, 61-62
Cooperative Extension Service, 88
Co-optation, and collaboration, 88-89
Coordination/control, as collaboration, 86, 90
Corporation for Public Broadcasting, 76
Cosponsorship, as collaboration, 86, 87-88, 89, 90-91
Costs: of collaboration, 93-94; and contract training, 66-67; of entry, low, and fragmentation, 20-21; leadership in, as generic strategy, 12-13; reducing, and collaboration, 89-90; as strategic variable, 8; of telecommunications, 81
Council on Postsecondary Accreditation, 76

D

Dallas Community College District, telecourses from, 76
Darkenwald, G., 86, 90, 94
Decentralization, and fragmentation, 25
Delaware, contract training in, 69

Delivery, context of, for continuing professional education, 46-47
Differentiation, as generic strategy, 13-14
Disneyland, as service provider, 40
Domain extension, and collaboration, 86-88
Donor relationships, as collaboration, 86, 90, 91
Dover Corporation, 37
Drucker, P. F., 6, 17

E

Economies of scale: for conglomerates, 32-33; creating, 26-27; and fragmentation, 21
Elderhostel: as collaboration, 99; fragmentation neutralized by, 27
Elliot, R. D., 26, 60, 65, 70
Evans, M. K., 33, 42
Extension strategies, by conglomerates, 39-40

F

Faculty: compensation of, in contract training, 67-68; and telecommunications, 80-81
Falk, C. F., 41, 42
Financial flexibility, as strategic variable, 9
Financial Redevelopment Act (Delaware), 69
Fischer, R. B., 2, 59, 60, 64, 70, 101
Flanking strategies, by conglomerates, 39
Focus. *See* Specialization
Foster, K., 37, 40, 43
Fox, K.F.A., 6, 17
Fragmented field: analysis of competition in, 19-29; background on, 19-20; competing in, 23-25; concept of, 20; and conglomerates, 36; neutralizing, 27-28; overcoming, 25-28; reasons for, 20-23; summary on, 28
Fred Pryor, and contract training, 59

G

Gale, B. T., 32, 33, 36, 37, 42
Gellman-Buzin, B., 2, 71, 83, 99

Geography: continuing professional education strategy for, 52-53; flexibility with, as strategic variable, 9; and fragmentation, 22, 24-25
Goals: and collaboration, 93; and continuing professional education, 45-46; and fragmentation, 23
Gronroos, C., 54, 57
Gup, B. E., 61, 70

H

Hammond, J. S., 6, 17
Harrison, W., 54, 58
Harvard University: and differentiation by reputation, 13; Institute for the Management of Lifelong Education of, 2
Heany, D. F., 36, 43
Hegarty, W. H., 6, 17
Henning, K. K., 57, 58
Heskett, J. L., 49, 50, 52, 58
Hohmann, L., 47, 58
Holiday Inn, and telecommunication, 74
Houle, C. O., 45, 46, 58

I

IBM, geographical inflexibility of, 9
Image of provider: and fragmentation, 23; as strategic variable, 7
Indiana/Purdue University Extension, flanking strategies of, 39
Innovation, by conglomerates, 38
Instruction, for conglomerates, 33-34
Integration effects, of conglomerates, 34-35

J

Johnson, D., 37, 40, 42

K

King, M. L., Jr., 42
Kissinger, H., 100, 101
Knowles, M., 100
Kotler, P., 6, 17, 32, 33, 34, 35, 37, 38, 39, 40, 42

L

Lasell Junior College, specialization by, 15

Learners, and fragmentation, 22-23
Learning Resources Network, and economies of scale, 26
Life-span integration, as strategic variable, 8
Logan, J. P., 6, 17
Lovelock, C. H., 6, 17, 39, 40, 42, 55, 58

M

McCallum, J. R., 54, 58
Machiavelli, N., 1
McKinsey and Co., 37
Market: power, of conglomerates, 33; segmentation and positioning for, 50-51
Marketing Science Institute, Profit Impact Market Strategy (PIMS) project of, 36, 37
Massachusetts Institute of Technology: and economies of scale, 26; and telecommunications, 75
Merson, J. C., 6, 17
Miami-Dade Community College, telecourses from, 76
Miller, P. A., 38, 40, 42-43
Minnesota, University of, as conglomerate, 32
Moses, S., 91, 94

N

National Technological University (NTU): and applications of telecommunications, 75, 82; and economies of scale, 26
National University Continuing Education Association, 64, 70
National University Teleconference Network (NUTN), and applications of telecommunications, 74-75, 82
New Jersey, collaboration in, 86, 90
New Mexico Tech Net, and fiber optics, 79
New York University, as conglomerate, 32
Newman, W. H., 6, 17
Normann, R., 55, 58

O

Oklahoma, statewide microwave in, 77-78

Oklahoma State Regents for Higher Education, 77
Oklahoma State University Educational Telecommunications Services, 74, 83

P

Pappas, J. P., 1, 31, 37, 40, 43, 98, 101
Parent organization relationship, as strategic variable, 9-10
Partnerships, for continuing professional education, 53
Pennsylvania State University, cable with microwave at, 78-79
Peters, T. J., 50, 58
Phillips, L. E., 45, 58
Planning: competitive, 49-55; strategic, 31-43, 80-82
Polytechnic Institute of New York, and telecommunications, 75
Porter, M. E., 6, 11, 16, 17, 20, 29, 49, 58
Pricing: by conglomerates, 35-36; fortification with, 37-38; and quality, 54-55; as strategic variable, 8-9; and value in contract training, 63
Proctor and Gamble, 37
Product development, by conglomerates, 35
Professional education. *See* Continuing professional education
Profit Impact Market Strategy (PIMS), 36, 37
Project ALLTEL, 76, 83
Promotion: by conglomerates, 40-41; as strategic variable, 7, 98-99
Providers: and fragmentation, 21-22, 23; goals of, 23, 45-46, 93; image of, 7, 23
Public Broadcasting Service, 76

Q

Quality: of conglomerates, 33-34, 39; in continuing professional education, 49-50, 54-55; emphasized, 100-101; and pricing 54-55
Qualls, R. L., 6, 17

R

Reciprocity, in collaboration, 92-93
Referral, as collaboration, 86, 89, 91
Regulation, and fragmentation, 21
Results orientation, for contract training, 62-63
Riccobono, J. A., 76, 83
Rio Grande Research Corridor, fiber optics in, 79
Risks: and collaboration, 90-91; as strategic variable, 7-8
Ryans, J. R., 6, 17

S

Scheuble, P. A., 33, 35, 43
Schoeffler, S., 36, 43
Services: by conglomerates, 40; excellence of, in continuing professional education, 49-50; and fragmentation, 25; as strategic variable, 9
Shanklin, W. L., 6, 17
Singleton, L. A., 72, 83
Smith, F., 88, 94
Smithsonian Institution, and differentiation by reputation, 13
Social responsiveness, of conglomerates, 41-42
Specialization: for continuing professional education, 51-52; and fragmentation, 24; as generic strategy, 14-16; as strategic variable, 7
Stanford University: Instructional Television Network (SITN) of, 79; and telecommunications, 75
State Higher Education Executive Officers, 76
Stern, M. R., 45, 46, 58
Strategic planning: in conglomerate continuing higher education, 31-43; for telecommunications, 80-82
Strategy. *See* Competitive strategy
Suleiman, A. S., 26, 41, 43
Sultan, G. M., 32, 33, 36, 37, 42

T

Taylor, J. W., 32, 33, 34, 35, 36, 37, 38, 43
Technological leadership, as strategic variable, 8
Telecommunications: analysis of, 71-83; background on, 71-72; conclusions on, 82-83; environment for, 73-74; literacy in, 72-73; national

applications of, 74-77; state and regional applications of, 77-80; strategic planning for, 80-82
Telecourses, in national applications, 75-77
Texas, statewide microwave in, 77, 78
Thomas A. Edison State College, fragmentation neutralized by, 27-28
Timeliness, of contract training, 62
Torbert, W. R., 100, 101
Training. *See* Contract training

U

Utah, University of: as conglomerate, 32; promotion by, 41, 98

V

Value, and pricing in contract training, 63

W

Warren, L. A., 91, 95
Waterman, R. H., Jr., 50, 58
Weinberg, C. B., 6, 17, 39, 40, 42
White Sands Missile Range, and fiber optics network, 79
Willard, J., 91, 95
Wind, Y. J., 33, 43
Wisconsin, University of, audioconferencing in, 78

Y

Young, W. H., 47, 57

Z

Zigerell, J., 78, 83